Connecting Re~~
Grades 5–6

MW01109647

Introduction..2
Features...3
Correlation Chart................................5
Fluency Checklist...............................6
Progress Record.................................7

🌐 **Lesson 1: It's Greek to Me!**
Connecting Background 8
Word Meaning Map 9
The Boy Who Cried Wolf 10
The Crow and the Snake 12
The Man and the Lion 14

⚛ **Lesson 2: Eek, Germs!**
Connecting Background 16
Making Inferences Chart...................17
Achoo! 18
Tummy Rumble................................20
Germ Superheroes 22

⚛ **Lesson 3: Survivors**
Connecting Background 24
Visualizing Web.................................25
What's Happening at the Beach? 26
What's Happening on the Plains? 28
What's Happening in the Winter? 30

⚛ **Lesson 4: From the Inside Out**
Connecting Background 32
Building Background Chart..................33
Your Brain 34
Your Nervous System 36
Your Digestive System 38

⚛ **Lesson 5: Alaska**
Connecting Background 40
Cause and Effect Charts 41
Musk Oxen 42
Glacier Bay National Park 44
Northern Lights...............................46

⚛ **Lesson 6: Change Is Good**
Connecting Background 48
Main Idea and Supporting Details
   Graphic Organizer 49
The Arctic Fox.................................50
The Anteater...................................52
The Polar Bear................................54

🌐 **Lesson 7: Who's Your Mummy?**
Connecting Background 56
Nonfiction Questions and Answers Chart....57
Mummy..58
The Pyramids 60
King Tut..62

⚛ **Les**
Conne~~................................... 64
Text Connections Web 65
A River of Ice 66
Oceans, Oceans, Everywhere 68
The Lifeline of the Southwest 70

🌐 **Lesson 9: Presidents Unite**
Connecting Background 72
Summarizing Chart 73
Teddy Bear Roosevelt......................74
Lincoln Goes to "Blab" School 76
George Washington's Teeth...............78

🌐 **Lesson 10: Fight for the Right**
Connecting Background 80
Sequence Chain 81
Evangeline Booth 82
Lewis Hine 84
Jane Addams..................................86

🌐 **Lesson 11: It's a Capital Idea!**
Connecting Background 88
Monitoring Comprehension Chart........89
Is the White House a Zoo?...............90
The Capitol Building.........................92
Arlington Heroes..............................94

🌐 **Lesson 12: Getting from Here to There**
Connecting Background 96
Problem and Solution Chart................97
The Erie Canal.................................98
The Mississippi Steamboats..............100
The Cumberland Road......................102

⚛ **Lesson 13: Dig It!**
Connecting Background 104
Drawing Conclusions Chart.................105
Pompeii 106
Jane 108
The Plain of Jars 110

⚛ **Lesson 14: Exciting Energy**
Connecting Background 112
Step Chart 113
Wind Powers a School 114
Using the Sun's Heat 116
Lowell National Historical Park...........118

🌐 **Lesson 15: Secrets in Stone**
Connecting Background 120
Main Idea and Supporting Details
   Graphic Organizer 121
Easter Island 122
Rosetta Stone.................................124
Stonehenge 126

Answer Key..................................128

Connecting Reading 5–6, SV 9781419036446

Introduction

Connecting Reading is a program that provides engaging fluency instruction for all of your readers. Students at different reading levels:

- Practice reading selections relating to the same topic.
- Pursue the same instructional goals.
- Interact and build fluency together.

Each lesson focuses on an interesting science or social studies topic. The three articles in each lesson have different reading levels as measured by the Flesch-Kincaid readability scale. Each student reads the selection most appropriate for him or her. Then students discuss the content of their articles. This mixed-ability grouping can promote meaningful interaction so that students build skills in a rich environment of peer-to-peer modeling, discussion, and feedback.

In addition, each passage includes the word count of each line. This provides an easy way to conduct timed readings with your students to assess reading speed.

Components

The following components are resources for the teacher.

- The **Correlation Chart** on page 5 is an easy reference that shows the reading skills, fluency skills, social studies standards, and science standards for each lesson.
- The **Fluency Checklist** on page 6 is a chart that students or teachers use to rate a reader's fluency performance, including word accuracy, rate, use of expression, and phrasing.
- The **Progress Record** is a timed assessment that calculates a student's reading rate. Given by the teacher, it can be used to determine a student's improvement during the year. You may wish to administer the assessment to different students each week.

The following components are part of each lesson.

- **Connecting Background** is a teacher resource that explains the focus skills in each lesson. It identifies the titles and levels of the three selections. The **Theme Notes** section explains how the articles are related and can be read aloud to students prior to beginning the lesson. The **Fluency Focus** explains the fluency skill students will work on, and a quick **Fluency Practice** can

be completed with the group to introduce the skill. The **Comprehension Focus** provides students with an opportunity to practice a reading skill using a nonfiction topic. Even though students are reading different articles, they all practice the same comprehension skill. Finally, a **vocabulary** list targets three words in each article that students may find challenging, either in pronunciation or contextual understanding.

- Each lesson also includes a **graphic organizer** to reinforce the comprehension skill.

- The **three articles** are short and interesting. The articles are leveled for different reading abilities. Students should read the selection that provides a slight challenge but still assures a successful reading experience. A **Fluency Tip** at the bottom of the page guides readers to a specific part of the text where they can practice the lesson's fluency skill.

- A **comprehension assessment** follows each article. Four multiple-choice questions check students' understanding. A fifth, inferential question requires students to respond in complete sentences.

Features

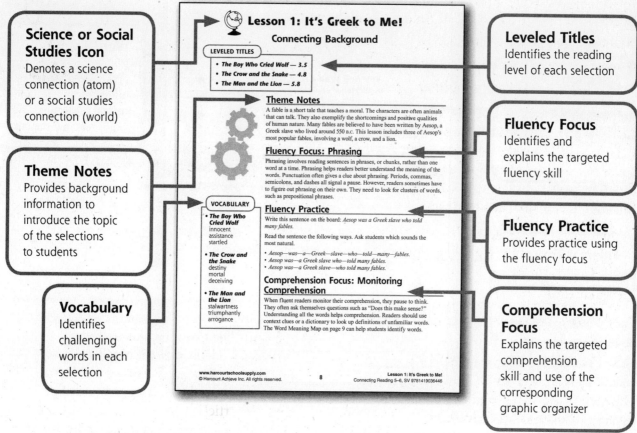

Science or Social Studies Icon
Denotes a science connection (atom) or a social studies connection (world)

Theme Notes
Provides background information to introduce the topic of the selections to students

Vocabulary
Identifies challenging words in each selection

Leveled Titles
Identifies the reading level of each selection

Fluency Focus
Identifies and explains the targeted fluency skill

Fluency Practice
Provides practice using the fluency focus

Comprehension Focus
Explains the targeted comprehension skill and use of the corresponding graphic organizer

Lesson 1: It's Greek to Me!
Connecting Background

LEVELED TITLES
- *The Boy Who Cried Wolf* — 3.5
- *The Crow and the Snake* — 4.8
- *The Man and the Lion* — 5.8

Theme Notes
A fable is a short tale that teaches a moral. The characters are often animals that can talk. They also exemplify the shortcomings and positive qualities of human nature. Many fables are believed to have been written by Aesop, a Greek slave who lived around 550 B.C. This lesson includes three of Aesop's most popular fables, involving a wolf, a crow, and a lion.

Fluency Focus: Phrasing
Phrasing involves reading sentences in phrases, or chunks, rather than one word at a time. Phrasing helps readers better understand the meaning of the words. Punctuation often gives a clue about phrasing. Periods, commas, semicolons, and dashes all signal a pause. However, readers sometimes have to figure out phrasing on their own. They need to look for clusters of words, such as prepositional phrases.

VOCABULARY
- *The Boy Who Cried Wolf*
  innocent
  assistance
  startled
- *The Crow and the Snake*
  destiny
  mortal
  deceiving
- *The Man and the Lion*
  stalwartness
  triumphantly
  arrogance

Fluency Practice
Write this sentence on the board: *Aesop was a Greek slave who told many fables.*

Read the sentence the following ways. Ask students which sounds the most natural.

- *Aesop—was—a—Greek—slave—who—told—many—fables.*
- *Aesop was—a Greek slave who—told many fables.*
- *Aesop was—a Greek slave—who told many fables.*

Comprehension Focus: Monitoring Comprehension
When fluent readers monitor their comprehension, they pause to think. They often ask themselves questions such as "Does this make sense?" Understanding all the words helps comprehension. Readers should use context clues or a dictionary to look up definitions of unfamiliar words. The Word Meaning Map on page 9 can help students identify words.

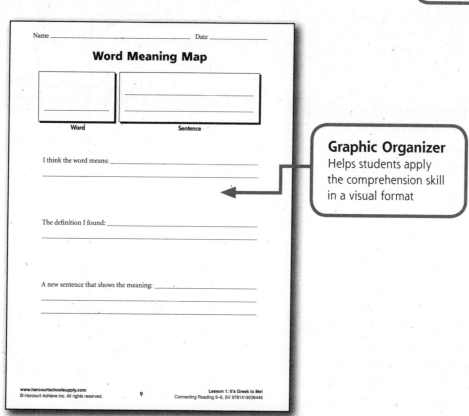

Name _____   Date _____

Word Meaning Map

Word	Sentence

I think the word means: _____

The definition I found: _____

A new sentence that shows the meaning: _____

Graphic Organizer
Helps students apply the comprehension skill in a visual format

Selection
Leveled passages can be used for fluency development or timed-reading assessment.

Fluency Tip
Explicit directions tell students how to apply the fluency focus to the selection.

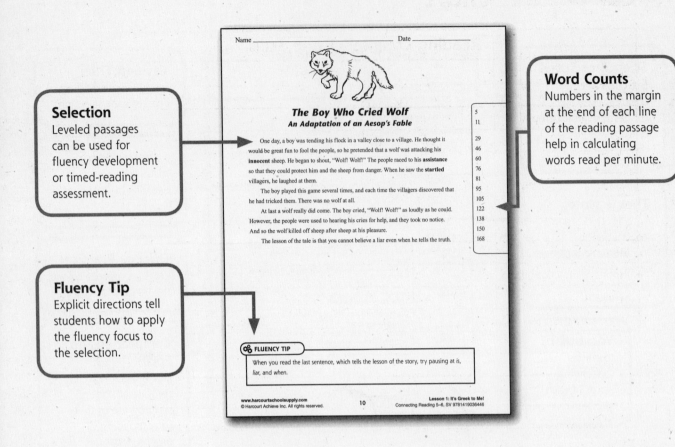

The Boy Who Cried Wolf
An Adaptation of an Aesop's Fable

One day, a boy was tending his flock in a valley close to a village. He thought it would be great fun to fool the people, so he pretended that a wolf was attacking his **innocent** sheep. He began to shout, "Wolf! Wolf!" The people raced to his **assistance** so that they could protect him and the sheep from danger. When he saw the **startled** villagers, he laughed at them.

The boy played this game several times, and each time the villagers discovered that he had tricked them. There was no wolf at all.

At last a wolf really did come. The boy cried, "Wolf! Wolf!" as loudly as he could. However, the people were used to hearing his cries for help, and they took no notice. And so the wolf killed off sheep after sheep at his pleasure.

The lesson of the tale is that you cannot believe a liar even when he tells the truth.

Word counts: 5, 11, 29, 46, 60, 76, 81, 95, 105, 122, 138, 150, 168

FLUENCY TIP

When you read the last sentence, which tells the lesson of the story, try pausing at *is*, *liar*, and *when*.

Word Counts
Numbers in the margin at the end of each line of the reading passage help in calculating words read per minute.

www.harcourtschoolsupply.com
© Harcourt Achieve Inc. All rights reserved.
10
Lesson 1: It's Greek to Me!
Connecting Reading 5–6, SV 9781419036446

Multiple-Choice Questions
Questions assess students' comprehension of the article using a test-like format.

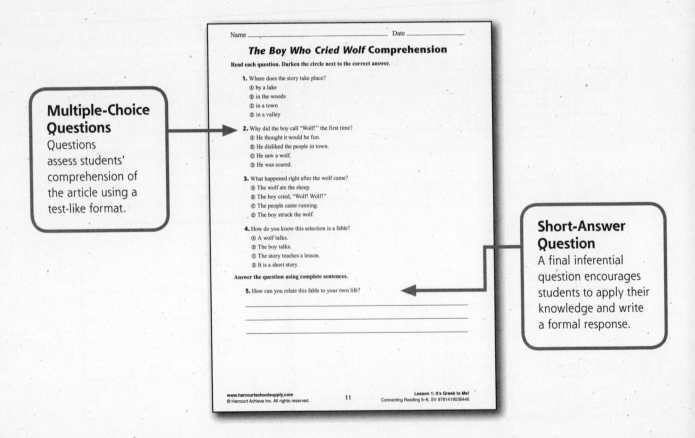

The Boy Who Cried Wolf Comprehension

Read each question. Darken the circle next to the correct answer.

1. Where does the story take place?
   Ⓐ by a lake
   Ⓑ in the woods
   Ⓒ in a town
   Ⓓ in a valley

2. Why did the boy call "Wolf!" the first time?
   Ⓐ He thought it would be fun.
   Ⓑ He disliked the people in town.
   Ⓒ He saw a wolf.
   Ⓓ He was scared.

3. What happened right after the wolf came?
   Ⓐ The wolf ate the sheep.
   Ⓑ The boy cried, "Wolf! Wolf!"
   Ⓒ The people came running.
   Ⓓ The boy struck the wolf.

4. How do you know this selection is a fable?
   Ⓐ A wolf talks.
   Ⓑ The boy talks.
   Ⓒ The story teaches a lesson.
   Ⓓ It is a short story.

Answer the question using complete sentences.

5. How can you relate this fable to your own life?

_____

_____

_____

Short-Answer Question
A final inferential question encourages students to apply their knowledge and write a formal response.

www.harcourtschoolsupply.com
© Harcourt Achieve Inc. All rights reserved.
11
Lesson 1: It's Greek to Me!
Connecting Reading 5–6, SV 9781419036446

www.harcourtschoolsupply.com
© Harcourt Achieve Inc. All rights reserved.

4

Features
Connecting Reading 5–6, SV 9781419036446

Correlation Chart

Reading Comprehension Skills

	Lessons
Asking questions	7
Building background	4
Cause and effect	5
Drawing conclusions	13
Main idea and supporting details	6, 15
Making connections	8
Making inferences	2
Monitoring comprehension	1, 11
Problem and solution	12
Sequence	10
Steps in a process	14
Summarizing	9
Visualizing	3

Fluency Skills

Expression	5, 6, 15
Phrasing	1, 7, 11, 14
Punctuation	2, 3, 9, 13
Word accuracy	4, 8, 10, 12

Science Standards

Describes the interactions between populations, natural disasters, and the environment	3
Describes some cycles, structures, and processes that are found in a system *Solar*	5, 8, 14
Identifies plant and animal adaptations	5, 6
Knows behavioral and structural adaptations that allow plants and animals to survive	5, 6
Knows the common characteristics of groups of animals	5, 6
Understands characteristics of weather	3, 14
Understands the relationships among various organisms and the environment	6
Understands how body systems interact	2, 4
Understands the role of solar energy in driving natural processes on Earth and in its atmosphere	14

Social Studies Standards

Understands the contributions of people of various racial, ethnic, and religious groups	1, 7, 10, 15
Understands the economic, political, cultural, and social processes that interact to shape patterns of human populations	7, 9, 12
Knows the characteristics and locations of important historical and contemporary societies	1, 7, 9, 11, 13, 15

Correlation Chart
Connecting Reading 5–6, SV 9781419036446

Name _____ Date _____

Fluency Checklist

Circle the number to rate the reading.

Selection title _____

	Very Good	Good	Needs to Improve
Word Reading Reads the words correctly	3	2	1
Rate of Reading Reads at a just-right rate— not too fast and not too slow	3	2	1
Expression Reads with expression	3	2	1
Phrasing Reads in groups of words— not word by word	3	2	1

Fluency Checklist
Connecting Reading 5–6, SV 9781419036446

Name _____ Date _____

Progress Record

Selection title _____

Oral Reading Rating Circle the rating that best describes the student's phrasing, adherence to author's syntax, and expressiveness. (4 is highest.)	4 3 2 1
Last Word Read _____ **Number of Words Read**	
Error Tally	—
Words Correct per Minute (WCPM) Score	=

Directions

1. Have a student read aloud the selection. Use a stopwatch or clock with a second hand to time the student. As the student reads, follow along on another photocopy of the story and unobtrusively make a mark in the Error Tally space for each error the student makes. Count mispronunciations, omissions, and substitutions as errors. Do not count repetitions or self-corrections as errors.

2. Have the student read the entire passage, but record the last word the student reads at the end of one minute. Alternatively, stop the student after one minute and record the last word read.

3. Rate the student's oral reading.

4. Use the last word read and the word count beside the last complete line read to determine the number of words read in one minute.

5. Subtract the error tally to calculate the WCPM score.

Progress Record
Connecting Reading 5–6, SV 9781419036446

Lesson 1: It's Greek to Me!
Connecting Background

LEVELED TITLES

- *The Boy Who Cried Wolf* — 3.5
- *The Crow and the Snake* — 4.8
- *The Man and the Lion* — 5.8

Theme Notes

A fable is a short tale that teaches a moral. The characters are often animals that can talk. They also exemplify the shortcomings and positive qualities of human nature. Many fables are believed to have been written by Aesop, a Greek slave who lived around 550 B.C. This lesson includes three of Aesop's most popular fables, involving a wolf, a crow, and a lion.

Fluency Focus: Phrasing

Phrasing involves reading sentences in phrases, or chunks, rather than one word at a time. Phrasing helps readers better understand the meaning of the words. Punctuation often gives a clue about phrasing. Periods, commas, semicolons, and dashes all signal a pause. However, readers sometimes have to figure out phrasing on their own. They need to look for clusters of words, such as prepositional phrases.

Fluency Practice

Write this sentence on the board: *Aesop was a Greek slave who told many fables.*

Read the sentence the following ways. Ask students which sounds the most natural.

- *Aesop—was—a—Greek—slave—who—told—many—fables.*
- *Aesop was—a Greek slave who—told many fables.*
- *Aesop was—a Greek slave—who told many fables.*

Comprehension Focus: Monitoring Comprehension

When fluent readers monitor their comprehension, they pause to think. They often ask themselves questions such as "Does this make sense?" Understanding all the words helps comprehension. Readers should use context clues or a dictionary to look up definitions of unfamiliar words. The Word Meaning Map on page 9 can help students identify words.

VOCABULARY

- **The Boy Who Cried Wolf**
  innocent
  assistance
  startled

- **The Crow and the Snake**
  destiny
  mortal
  deceiving

- **The Man and the Lion**
  stalwartness
  triumphantly
  arrogance

Name _____ Date _____

Word Meaning Map

_____	_____
	_____
Word	**Sentence**

I think the word means: _____

_____

The definition I found: _____

_____

A new sentence that shows the meaning: _____

_____

_____

Connecting Reading 5–6, SV 9781419036446

Name _____ Date _____

The Boy Who Cried Wolf
An Adaptation of an Aesop's Fable

One day, a boy was tending his flock in a valley close to a village. He thought it
would be great fun to fool the people, so he pretended that a wolf was attacking his
innocent sheep. He began to shout, "Wolf! Wolf!" The people raced to his **assistance**
so that they could protect him and the sheep from danger. When he saw the **startled**
villagers, he laughed at them.

The boy played this game several times, and each time the villagers discovered that
he had tricked them. There was no wolf at all.

At last a wolf really did come. The boy cried, "Wolf! Wolf!" as loudly as he could.
However, the people were used to hearing his cries for help, and they took no notice.
And so the wolf killed off sheep after sheep at his pleasure.

The lesson of the tale is that you cannot believe a liar even when he tells the truth.

5
11
29
46
60
76
81
95
105
122
138
150
168

⚙ FLUENCY TIP

When you read the last sentence, which tells the lesson of the story, try pausing at *is*,
liar, and *when*.

Connecting Reading 5–6, SV 9781419036446

Name _____ Date _____

The Boy Who Cried Wolf Comprehension

Read each question. Darken the circle next to the correct answer.

1. Where does the story take place?

    Ⓐ by a lake

    Ⓑ in the woods

    Ⓒ in a town

    Ⓓ in a valley

2. Why did the boy call "Wolf!" the first time?

    Ⓐ He thought it would be fun.

    Ⓑ He disliked the people in town.

    Ⓒ He saw a wolf.

    Ⓓ He was scared.

3. What happened right after the wolf came?

    Ⓐ The wolf ate the sheep.

    Ⓑ The boy cried, "Wolf! Wolf!"

    Ⓒ The people came running.

    Ⓓ The boy struck the wolf.

4. How do you know this selection is a fable?

    Ⓐ A wolf talks.

    Ⓑ The boy talks.

    Ⓒ The story teaches a lesson.

    Ⓓ It is a short story.

Answer the question using complete sentences.

5. How can you relate this fable to your own life?

    _____

    _____

    _____

Lesson 1: It's Greek to Me!
Connecting Reading 5–6, SV 9781419036446

The Crow and the Snake
An Adaptation of an Aesop's Fable

One day, a crow perched on a tree branch and thought about his **destiny**. "I am such a wise bird, so I'm positive that my destiny is to be great and powerful," he exclaimed. "Look at this glorious world. The earth is brimming with delicious things to eat and sweet water to drink. Goodness is everywhere I look."

Suddenly, the hungry crow spied a snake lying stretched out in a sunny spot. Thinking it was dead, the crow swiftly flew down, snatched it up in his claws, and soared up to the sky. He carried the snake to a hideaway where he could dine on it without being disturbed. Just as the crow was about to feast, the snake reared its head and struck the crow with its fangs.

Since the snake was poisonous, the bite was a **mortal** wound. The crow wondered to himself, "Is this my destiny?" The dying crow then said, "Oh, what a severe twist of fate! I thought I had made a fortunate discovery, but instead, this choice has cost me my life!"

The lesson of this tale is that appearances can be extremely **deceiving**.

5
11
28
45
61
69
83
100
119
137
140
155
172
189
201

⚙ FLUENCY TIP

Look at the last line in the third paragraph. Reread it to a partner, pausing after *discovery*, *instead*, and *choice*.

The Crow and the Snake Comprehension

Read each question. Darken the circle next to the correct answer.

1. What do you think the crow is like?

Ⓐ generous

Ⓑ proud

Ⓒ kind

Ⓓ mean

2. What happened after the crow flew away with the snake?

Ⓐ He dropped the snake.

Ⓑ He ate the snake.

Ⓒ He perched on a branch.

Ⓓ He took the snake to a hideaway.

3. In this story, what does *mortal* mean?

Ⓐ human

Ⓑ deadly

Ⓒ painful

Ⓓ itchy

4. What was the crow's "severe twist of fate"?

Ⓐ He was going to die.

Ⓑ He found a snake.

Ⓒ He was hungry.

Ⓓ The snake got away.

Answer the question using complete sentences.

5. What important detail in the first paragraph gave you a clue about what might happen?

_____

_____

_____

The Man and the Lion
An Adaptation of an Aesop's Fable

	5
	11

A man and a lion befriended each other. Because they were good pals, they decided 26
to go on a journey together. Each enjoyed the other's company immensely, and they 40
passionately discussed worldly concerns. In the course of conversation, they began to boast 53
of their prowess, and each asserted that he was superior to the other in intense strength 69
and personal courage. Each gave examples of his personal **stalwartness**. They were still 82
having their dispute when they came to a crossroad where there was a statue of a man 99
strangling a lion. 102

"There!" said the man **triumphantly**. "Feast your eyes on that! Doesn't that prove to 116
you that a man is stronger than a lion?" 125

"Not so fast, my comrade," exclaimed the lion. "Do not let your **arrogance** affect your 140
perception. You are too quick to reach a verdict. If we lions could make statues, you may be 158
sure that in most of them you would see the man underneath." 170

The lesson of this tale is that there are two sides to every question. 184

⚙️ **FLUENCY TIP**

The fourth sentence is long. Reread it to a partner, pausing after *conversation*, *prowess*, and *other*.

Connecting Reading 5–6, SV 9781419036446

The Man and the Lion Comprehension

Read each question. Darken the circle next to the correct answer.

1. Why did the man and lion take a journey?

   Ⓐ They wanted to see who was stronger.

   Ⓑ They had to ask the king a question.

   Ⓒ They were friends.

   Ⓓ They went to see a statue.

2. What might the lion say was his personal stalwartness?

   Ⓐ his claws

   Ⓑ his mane

   Ⓒ his tail

   Ⓓ his roar

3. What happens after the friends see the statue?

   Ⓐ The man claims he is better.

   Ⓑ The lion claims he is better.

   Ⓒ The friends pose like the statue.

   Ⓓ The lion makes a statue to show his view.

4. Why would a lion make a statue with a man on the bottom?

   Ⓐ because a man is smaller in size

   Ⓑ because it shows the lion's opinion that he is stronger

   Ⓒ because both friends agree the lion is stronger

   Ⓓ because a man is stronger and should be on the bottom

Answer the question using complete sentences.

5. Who do you think is stronger, the man or the lion? Explain.

_____

_____

_____

Lesson 2: Eek, Germs!
Connecting Background

LEVELED TITLES

- *Achoo!* — 4.0
- *Tummy Rumble* — 5.1
- *Germ Superheroes* — 6.0

Theme Notes

There are billions of germs in our world. In fact, right now, there are probably millions of them on the skin of every person. This lesson covers the topics of infection, bad bacteria, and good bacteria.

Fluency Focus: Punctuation

Fluent readers pay attention to punctuation. They read based on the punctuation. For example, readers should pause at commas and dashes, stop at periods, raise their voice at question marks, and express excitement at exclamation points.

Fluency Practice

Write this sentence on the board: *Germs can enter the body through the nose, the mouth, or a cut on the skin, causing an infection.*

Point out the commas and model reading the sentence with and without pauses. Discuss which sounds like natural speech. Invite partners to take turns reading the sentence.

Comprehension Focus: Making Inferences

An author does not always tell everything in the text. Readers must look at the information or facts and then think about what they already know from personal experience that relates to the topic. By putting all the information together, readers can understand ideas that are not directly stated. Students will be able to make inferences using the Making Inferences Chart on page 17.

VOCABULARY

- *Achoo!*
  infection
  virus
  germs

- *Tummy Rumble*
  bacteria
  viruses
  organisms

- *Germ Superheroes*
  bacteria
  intestines
  vaccines

www.harcourtschoolsupply.com
© Harcourt Achieve Inc. All rights reserved.

16

Lesson 2: Eek, Germs!
Connecting Reading 5–6, SV 9781419036446

Name _____ Date _____

Making Inferences Chart

What I Know	Information in the Selection	What I Infer

Achoo!

	1

Your throat is scratchy and sore, and you are sneezing frequently—achoo, achoo! Soon | 15
your nose starts to drip, drip, drip. Your head might be throbbing, too, because it is stuffed | 32
up. You have acquired an **infection** known as the common cold. | 43

Colds come from a germ called a **virus**. Kids catch between three and eight colds | 58
a year. So how did you catch your last cold? Well, you might have touched a doorknob, | 75
telephone, or coin. **Germs** can live on objects for a long time, and when you touch the | 92
objects, the germs are transferred to your hands. Then you probably ate lunch without | 106
washing your hands. You actually ate some of those germs! Now, don't you agree that's | 121
really gross? | 123

You also can get germs from people who sneeze and cough in your direction. The | 138
germs in those droplets spread out and travel invisibly through the air. People should be | 153
careful to sneeze and cough into a tissue or, at least, their arms, so that others don't come | 171
into contact with the germs. Keep that germ spray out of the air and off your hands, and | 189
then you will probably avoid those germs and remain healthy! | 199

⚙ FLUENCY TIP

Use your voice to show excitement at those exclamation points!

Name _____ Date _____

Achoo! Comprehension

Read each question. Darken the circle next to the correct answer.

1. Which is NOT a sign of a cold?

Ⓐ a sore throat

Ⓑ a runny nose

Ⓒ an aching stomach

Ⓓ sneezing

2. What causes a cold?

Ⓐ a virus

Ⓑ medicine

Ⓒ washing hands

Ⓓ playing with food

3. What happens after people sneeze?

Ⓐ They cough.

Ⓑ Drops spread out.

Ⓒ They get a cold.

Ⓓ Their nose tickles.

4. Why should people cough into a tissue?

Ⓐ It keeps the germs from flying through the air.

Ⓑ It stops the cough.

Ⓒ It kills the germs.

Ⓓ It makes people get well faster.

Answer the question using complete sentences.

5. What is the most important thing you can do to keep from getting a cold? Explain.

_____

_____

_____

Lesson 2: Eek, Germs!
Connecting Reading 5–6, SV 9781419036446

Tummy Rumble

	2

You had a pleasant dinner and went to bed feeling fine. All of a sudden, you wake up in | 21

the middle of the night. You feel your tummy rumble with horrible pains. It is time to get to | 40

the bathroom—quick! You may have food poisoning! | 48

All food has **bacteria** in it. Food poisoning comes from eating food with bad bacteria, | 63

viruses, or parasites. Some food may be spoiled, or it may not be cooked properly. | 78

Food poisoning is often caused by foods that come from animals, such as meat, fish, | 93

or eggs. These foods need to be cooked well to kill the bad bacteria. Before milk is sold, it | 112

needs to be heated to kill the harmful **organisms**, too. | 122

To protect yourself, make sure that hot foods stay hot and cold foods stay cold. Reheat | 138

leftovers until they are steaming. | 143

Almost five thousand people in the United States die from food poisoning every year, | 157

so be careful that you eat properly prepared food. | 166

⚙️ FLUENCY TIP

Take a short breath after end punctuation, or you might run out of air in the wrong place!

Connecting Reading 5–6, SV 9781419036446

Tummy Rumble Comprehension

Read each question. Darken the circle next to the correct answer.

1. What is another name for *tummy*?

Ⓐ heart

Ⓑ intestines

Ⓒ stomach

Ⓓ lungs

2. What do milk producers do before selling it?

Ⓐ freeze it

Ⓑ heat it

Ⓒ melt it

Ⓓ drink it

3. What causes food poisoning?

Ⓐ good viruses

Ⓑ heated food

Ⓒ cold milk

Ⓓ bad bacteria

4. How do you know if leftover pizza is safe to eat?

Ⓐ It is green.

Ⓑ It is steaming.

Ⓒ It is cold.

Ⓓ It is in the box.

Answer the question using complete sentences.

5. What does cooking food thoroughly do to germs?

_____

_____

_____

Germ Superheroes

| | 2 |

     Not all **bacteria** are created equal. Bad bacteria can make us sick. However, good | 16

bacteria can do amazing, and sometimes, delicious things. | 24

     Did you know that bacteria are important to farmers? Some farmers use bacteria to | 38

fertilize the soil. Bacteria help grow crops. Farmers also use bacteria to kill bugs. This is a | 55

natural way to get rid of pests. | 62

     Some foods are made with the help of bacteria. Buttermilk, yogurt, and cheese | 75

are examples. | 77

     In sewage plants, bacteria are used to break down human waste. Without bacteria, the | 91

waste would pile up. Our world would not be healthy. There are bacteria in your body, too. | 108

Bacteria live in your **intestines**. Bacteria break down the waste before it leaves your body. | 123

     Bacteria can also be used to make medicines and **vaccines**. Scientists are on the | 137

lookout for other good uses for bacteria. | 144

⚙ **FLUENCY TIP**

Watch for commas in the third sentence. Make sure to pause at each comma.

Name _____ Date _____

Germ Superheroes Comprehension

Read each question. Darken the circle next to the correct answer.

1. How do farmers use bacteria?

Ⓐ They feed bacteria to animals.

Ⓑ They fertilize soil with bacteria.

Ⓒ They use bacteria as fuel in tractors.

Ⓓ They grow bacteria as a crop.

2. Why is a natural bug killer good?

Ⓐ It kills only the harmful bugs.

Ⓑ It changes crops so bugs won't eat them.

Ⓒ It is safe for the environment.

Ⓓ It lasts only a short while.

3. How do you know that good bacteria are in yogurt?

Ⓐ Yogurt breaks down in the intestine.

Ⓑ Yogurt is a healthy food to eat.

Ⓒ Yogurt makes you sick.

Ⓓ Yogurt changes food into waste.

4. What is a vaccine?

Ⓐ a kind of fertilizer

Ⓑ a process that breaks food into smaller parts

Ⓒ a kind of delicious food

Ⓓ a medicine given in the form of a shot

Answer the question using complete sentences.

5. Why did the author use the title "Germ Superheroes" for this article?

_____

_____

_____

Lesson 3: Survivors
Connecting Background

LEVELED TITLES

- *What's Happening at the Beach?* — 4.1
- *What's Happening on the Plains?* — 5.3
- *What's Happening in the Winter?* — 6.1

Theme Notes

Disasters can strike in minutes. In some places, a specific kind of event might be expected to happen on occasion, such as a blizzard in the northern parts of the United States. It is always a good idea to recognize the signs of the event and know what to do. The three readings in this lesson use a multiple-choice format to cover the topics of tsunamis, tornadoes, and blizzards.

Fluency Focus: Punctuation

Fluent readers use punctuation to help them understand and remember what they read. A question mark means something is being asked, so the reader raises the level of the voice at the end of the sentence. If a sentence is long, paying attention to the punctuation will help break up the sentence into smaller, more understandable parts.

Fluency Practice

Write these words on the board: *A man stood by the window of the burning building what was he going to do before long we saw him jump to safety*

Ask partners to rewrite the words to make complete sentences. Then have them practice reading them fluently.

Comprehension Focus: Visualizing

Visualizing means that readers use the words they read or hear to paint pictures in their minds. These pictures help them imagine what a character, a place, or a thing looks like. Visualizing will help readers understand and remember what they read. The Visualizing Web on page 25 can help students better visualize the information in each text.

VOCABULARY

- *What's Happening at the Beach?*
  stable
  situation
  fragments

- *What's Happening on the Plains?*
  thunderous
  foresight
  durable

- *What's Happening in the Winter?*
  exhaustion
  accumulation
  flustered

Name _____ Date _____

Visualizing Web

Word or phrase clue:

Word or phrase clue:

The picture I visualize:

Word or phrase clue:

Word or phrase clue:

Connecting Reading 5–6, SV 9781419036446

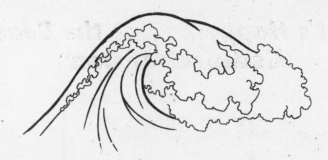

What's Happening at the Beach?

| | 5 |

Imagine that you live at the beach and that you are playing along the shore on a | 22
sunny day. Suddenly, the ground begins to rumble, rattle, and shake. When the ground is | 37
stable again, you look out at the water and see that the water's edge has changed. It's way | 55
out in the distance where some of the bigger waves usually start breaking. The water stays | 71
there 5, 10, 15 seconds. What's happening? | 78

    a. The tide is changing. | 83

    b. A tsunami is coming. | 88

    c. It's going to rain. | 93

The correct answer is **b**, because the earth's movement signals that an earthquake | 106
has occurred. Earthquakes deep under the ocean floor can cause a tsunami. A tsunami is a | 122
huge wave of water that can rise higher than a building several stories tall. What should you | 139
do in this **situation**? | 143

    a. Stay where you are. | 148

    b. Go in the house. | 153

    c. Run for higher ground. | 158

The correct answer is **c**. If you remain at the beach, you most likely will be | 174
drowned and washed out to sea. If your house is near the beach, it will probably be | 191
destroyed, too. The tsunami is so powerful that it can smash a brick and wood structure into | 208
hundreds of **fragments**. | 211

⚙ FLUENCY TIP

Try pausing a bit more than usual after the periods in each sentence in the first paragraph. It will add interest and gain your audience's attention.

Lesson 3: Survivors
Connecting Reading 5–6, SV 9781419036446

Name _____   Date _____

What's Happening at the Beach?
Comprehension

Read each question. Darken the circle next to the correct answer.

1. In this story, what is the "rumble, rattle, and shake"?

    Ⓐ a tornado

    Ⓑ an earthquake

    Ⓒ a seasonal change

    Ⓓ a volcano

2. If a tsunami is coming, what happens after the ground shakes?

    Ⓐ Buildings fall down.

    Ⓑ People collect shells.

    Ⓒ The water moves away from the shore.

    Ⓓ It begins to rain.

3. Where do tsunamis happen?

    Ⓐ in the mountains

    Ⓑ along a riverbank

    Ⓒ by the ocean

    Ⓓ in the desert

4. Why should you leave an area if you think a tsunami might hit?

    Ⓐ Buildings will fall.

    Ⓑ Mud will slide.

    Ⓒ Fish will bite.

    Ⓓ You can drown.

Answer the question using complete sentences.

5. Describe how you think the water looks right before a tsunami.

_____

_____

_____

Connecting Reading 5–6, SV 9781419036446

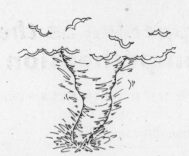

What's Happening on the Plains?

Imagine that you are outside doing chores on the plains. It is about 5:00 in the evening, and you notice that the sky is dark and appears green. The wind has completely stopped blowing. As you walk toward the house, tremendous hailstones begin falling. You hear a **thunderous** roar, like a giant freight train is approaching. What's happening?

a. A bomb exploded.

b. A tsunami is about to strike.

c. A tornado is about to appear.

The correct answer is **c**, because the changes you experienced are all indicators of a tornado. You need to find shelter immediately. Where do you go in this situation?

a. You crouch under a tree.

b. You run into a basement or interior room.

c. You hide in your car.

The correct answer is **b**. If you live in tornado country, you know the other choices can be deadly. You've probably had the **foresight** to identify a safe place to go. Underground is the safest place to be. An interior room inside your house is the next best thing because there are no windows. Hunker down under a **durable** piece of furniture and wait it out.

5
21
37
50
63
67
74
81
95
110
116
125
131
147
163
181
197

⚙ FLUENCY TIP

Find the sentences that end in question marks. Look ahead so you can change your voice when you read a question.

What's Happening on the Plains?
Comprehension

Read each question. Darken the circle next to the correct answer.

1. Which is NOT a clue that a tornado is coming?

Ⓐ freight train sounds

Ⓑ hail

Ⓒ green sky

Ⓓ birds squawking

2. Where do tornadoes most often strike?

Ⓐ in a hilly place

Ⓑ in a wet place

Ⓒ in a cold place

Ⓓ in a flat place

3. Which is the best place to be in a tornado?

Ⓐ underwater

Ⓑ in an upstairs bedroom

Ⓒ in the basement

Ⓓ under a tree

4. If you *hunker down*, what are you doing?

Ⓐ taking shelter under something

Ⓑ climbing up into something

Ⓒ turning on something

Ⓓ moving something

Answer the question using complete sentences.

5. Why is it a good idea to be in an interior room if a tornado strikes?

_____

_____

_____

What's Happening in the Winter?

	5

Imagine that it's the middle of the night in extremely cold temperatures. You've been driving for hours and are close to **exhaustion**. You find a spot along a secluded road where you can pull over and rest for several hours. When you awaken, the wind is blowing so brutally that it's shaking your vehicle. It's completely white outside, and you can't see more than a few inches in front of you. What's happening?

a. You are trapped in a blizzard.

b. A snowplow has pushed snow onto your vehicle.

c. Pranksters have covered your car with snow.

The correct answer is **a**. A blizzard is defined as a large **accumulation** of snow with winds blasting in excess of 35 miles per hour. In a blizzard, visibility is practically zero. What should you do in this situation?

a. Abandon your vehicle immediately.

b. Remain in your vehicle.

c. Get out of your vehicle, but stay in the vicinity.

The correct answer is **b**. It's easy to get **flustered** and disoriented in the extreme cold when there is wind-driven snow. If you remain in your vehicle, it's more probable that rescuers will locate you. To keep from freezing to death, run the engine for about ten minutes each hour, but be sure to open the window a crack to avoid carbon monoxide poisoning.

18
35
52
67
78
85
94
102
117
133
141
146
151
162
176
191
206
224
226

⚙ FLUENCY TIP

Look at the choices written in a testing format. Pause after each period and each item. For example, *a.* [pause] *You are trapped in a blizzard.* [pause] *b.* [pause]…

Connecting Reading 5–6, SV 9781419036446

Name _____ Date _____

What's Happening in the Winter?
Comprehension

Read each question. Darken the circle next to the correct answer.

1. In this scene, where are you?

Ⓐ in a house

Ⓑ in a restaurant

Ⓒ in a car

Ⓓ on a snowplow

2. Why can't someone see in the distance in a blizzard?

Ⓐ It is night, so it is too dark.

Ⓑ Heavy snow is falling.

Ⓒ The rain made ice on the window.

Ⓓ The plow is in the way.

3. If you are *disoriented*, how are you feeling?

Ⓐ happy

Ⓑ angry

Ⓒ confused

Ⓓ sure

4. Why should you turn on the car for ten minutes each hour?

Ⓐ to run the heat for warmth

Ⓑ to blow the horn to alert rescuers

Ⓒ to move air for breathing

Ⓓ to have energy to play the radio

Answer the question using complete sentences.

5. What pictures did you form in your mind as you read the passage?

_____

_____

_____

Lesson 3: Survivors
Connecting Reading 5–6, SV 9781419036446

Lesson 4: From the Inside Out

Connecting Background

LEVELED TITLES

- *Your Brain* — 4.1
- *Your Nervous System* — 5.4
- *Your Digestive System* — 6.2

Theme Notes

The human body is an amazing machine. It is made up of organs, muscles, tissues, and fluids that form different systems. In this lesson, readers take fantasy trips inside the brain, the nervous system, and the digestive system to learn about the workings of the body.

Fluency Focus: Word Accuracy

Fluent readers read with accuracy. They learn how to pronounce difficult words, and they learn what the words mean. They do not skip or add words. When reading, it is important to sound out each word and to think about whether the text makes sense.

Fluency Practice

Write these sentences on the board: *The human body is a grape machine. Some of the my parts can move all by themselves. We have think to move others.*

Explain that each sentence contains a mistake. Have students write the sentences correctly by adding, changing, or removing a word. Then encourage them to practice reading the corrected sentences fluently.

Comprehension Focus: Building Background

When fluent readers build background, they make connections between what they read and what they know. Sometimes the text reminds them of a personal experience or makes them think about something they already know about the world. Building background helps them think about a topic so they can better understand the text. Readers can build background by looking at pictures in the article and reading the title. The graphic organizer on page 33 can help students build background.

VOCABULARY

- *Your Brain*
  unique
  appearance
  disgusting

- *Your Nervous System*
  network
  receptors
  appropriate

- *Your Digestive System*
  anticipate
  poised
  extracted

Name _____ Date _____

Building Background Chart

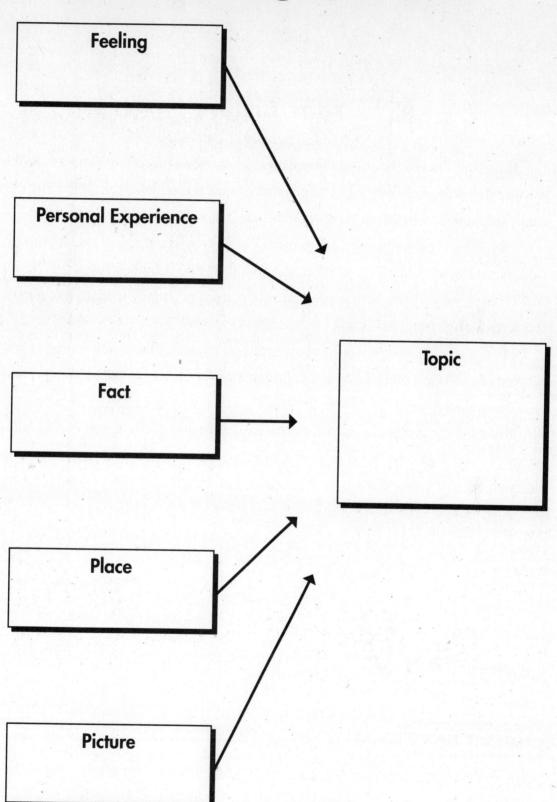

Lesson 4: From the Inside Out
Connecting Reading 5–6, SV 9781419036446

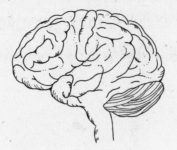

Your Brain

	2

Heads up! I'm your brain—a **unique** organ in every way. I control almost everything you do every second of every day. I help you remember a good joke, run a race, and smell stinky sneakers. Ick! In fact, right now I'm helping you read and understand this page!

I weigh nearly three pounds. An elephant's brain weighs more than twelve pounds. Does that mean an elephant can think bigger thoughts? I don't think so!

I'm wet and gray and have the **appearance** of a soggy, muddy sponge. You may think that sounds **disgusting**, but I think I'm actually very pretty.

I'm made up of about 100 billion nerve cells, or neurons. How many is that? If you counted one cell each second, you would be counting for over 3,171 years! You probably have better things to do!

I look out for you, so please look out for me. Eat healthy foods, exercise daily, and get plenty of sleep. And don't forget to wear your helmet when you participate in contact sports, ride your bike, or in-line skate. Now that's using your head!

17
36
51
64
77
93
103
120
135
140
158
174
185

⚙ FLUENCY TIP

Look at the science words on this page, such as *brain*, *cells*, and *neurons*. Read them carefully so you don't say the wrong word.

Name _____ Date _____

Your Brain Comprehension

Read each question. Darken the circle next to the correct answer.

1. What is the main job of the brain?
   - Ⓐ to move the legs
   - Ⓑ to feed the body
   - Ⓒ to control the body
   - Ⓓ to grow hair

2. About how much does the brain weigh?
   - Ⓐ twelve pounds
   - Ⓑ three pounds
   - Ⓒ one hundred pounds
   - Ⓓ three thousand pounds

3. Which is NOT a way to keep the brain healthy?
   - Ⓐ eating good foods
   - Ⓑ getting lots of sleep
   - Ⓒ exercising daily
   - Ⓓ reading as little as possible

4. Why should you wear a helmet when you ride your bike?
   - Ⓐ to keep the brain from falling out when you go fast
   - Ⓑ to keep from hitting the head and hurting the brain
   - Ⓒ to keep the brain from swelling in the heat
   - Ⓓ to keep the brain warm when it is cold outside

Answer the question using complete sentences.

5. When did you use your brain to do the right thing?

_____

_____

_____

Connecting Reading 5–6, SV 9781419036446

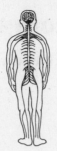

Your Nervous System

3

21
39
57
59
72
89
91
103
119
133
135
147
162
175

Think about all the things you can do! You can catch a whiff of burnt toast or taste a salty chip. You can hear a loud crack of thunder and pick at your fingernail. Do you remember the best thing about last Friday? You can laugh or cry. Every once in a while you even think!

These experiences are brought to you by your nervous system. Your nervous system consists of your brain, spinal cord, and a vast **network** of nerves. It serves as your body's command center.

Here's how it works. **Receptors** constantly recognize changes inside and outside your body. Outside receptors such as your eyes, ears, and skin notice changes in light, sound, and temperature. Inside receptors such as your heart and stomach sense changes in chemicals and body fluids.

Instantly, your receptors send their information through your nerves and spinal cord and into your brain. Quickly, your brain processes the information and sends a command to the **appropriate** body part. Your body reacts, and life goes on as always!

⚙ FLUENCY TIP

The last two paragraphs have some difficult words. Practice reading *receptors*, *chemicals*, and *appropriate* so you don't say the wrong word by mistake.

Name _____ Date _____

Your Nervous System Comprehension

Read each question. Darken the circle next to the correct answer.

1. Which is NOT a job of the nervous system?

Ⓐ to smell food

Ⓑ to see colors

Ⓒ to pump blood

Ⓓ to feel objects

2. Which is part of the nervous system?

Ⓐ brain

Ⓑ stomach

Ⓒ heart

Ⓓ bone

3. Where does the information go after it moves through the nerves?

Ⓐ to the brain

Ⓑ to the ears

Ⓒ to the skin

Ⓓ to the spinal cord

4. Why does the article say the nervous system is the command center?

Ⓐ It tells the body how to react.

Ⓑ It takes orders to know how to move.

Ⓒ It is in the center of the body.

Ⓓ It gives energy to the whole body.

Answer the question using complete sentences.

5. What might happen if the nervous system got the wrong information from your eyes? Explain.

_____

_____

_____

Lesson 4: From the Inside Out
Connecting Reading 5–6, SV 9781419036446

Your Digestive System

| | 3 |

You **anticipate** the satisfying flavor of a cherry before it touches your lips. Plucking it | 18
from its stem, you balance it on your tongue. Then what? | 29

Then your teeth grind the cherry into bits, signaling your salivary glands to gush | 43
saliva, or spit, which dampens the morsels. And, presto, you've produced a moist ball of | 58
cherry mush **poised** on your tongue. Yum! | 65

Within seconds, your tongue propels the mush to the back of your throat, flinging it | 80
swiftly down your esophagus, or gullet. As the muscles of your esophagus squeeze the wet | 95
mass downward, a valve in your stomach opens. | 103

And plop! The mass of mush finds itself sloshing around with mucus and stomach | 117
juices, transformed into a thick fluid called chyme.* | 125

As chyme rambles through your small intestines, nutrients are **extracted**, absorbed by | 137
your bloodstream, and delivered throughout your body. | 144

But this adventure's not over! The waste that your body can't utilize is dumped into | 159
your large intestines, where the water is removed, and the resulting solids are passed from | 174
your body. Now that's the end! | 180

* (KIME)

⚙ **FLUENCY TIP**

Before you read, look for any difficult words and be sure you can say them. Then you'll
be able to read without errors.

Connecting Reading 5–6, SV 9781419036446

Name _____ Date _____

Your Digestive System Comprehension

Read each question. Darken the circle next to the correct answer.

1. What does the digestive system do?

Ⓐ It helps you see.

Ⓑ It gets nutrients for your body.

Ⓒ It makes the stomach healthy.

Ⓓ It makes more blood.

2. Where does food go right before it enters the small intestine?

Ⓐ mouth

Ⓑ large intestine

Ⓒ stomach

Ⓓ esophagus

3. What breaks down the food in the stomach?

Ⓐ blood

Ⓑ juices

Ⓒ morsels

Ⓓ water

4. Why does saliva soften the food?

Ⓐ to help it move easily down the esophagus

Ⓑ to take out the waste

Ⓒ to add more water

Ⓓ to add nutrients

Answer the question using complete sentences.

5. Should you make food choices based on taste or on nutritional value? Explain.

_____

_____

_____

Lesson 4: From the Inside Out
Connecting Reading 5–6, SV 9781419036446

Lesson 5: Alaska
Connecting Background

Theme Notes

Alaska is considered to be one of the few remaining frontiers for people to explore. Its winters are harsh, due to freezing temperatures and lack of sunlight. However, because it is so wild, many sites are clear and natural. The three topics in this lesson focus on some fascinating aspects of Alaska—Glacier Bay National Park, the northern lights, and musk oxen.

Fluency Focus: Expression

Fluent readers use expression. They stress key words in a sentence to make the reading interesting and show what is important. Expression can also give different meanings to a sentence. Expressive reading means using a higher voice to end questions and saying important words longer, louder, or with a different voice.

Fluency Practice

Write this sentence on the board: *Mom says that we are going to Alaska for vacation.*

Ask partners to read the sentence three times—to show sadness, happiness, and excitement.

Comprehension Focus: Cause and Effect

A cause is something that happens. An effect is what happens as a result of the cause. Some clue words that show cause and effect relationships include *because, since, thus, so,* and *as a result.* Sometimes, one cause can have several effects. The Cause and Effect Charts on page 41 can help students identify the cause and effect relationships in each selection.

VOCABULARY

- *Musk Oxen*
  survival
  bitter
  tundra

- *Glacier Bay National Park*
  bitter
  glaciers
  towering

- *Northern Lights*
  stupendous
  phenomenon
  collide

Connecting Reading 5–6, SV 9781419036446

Name _____ Date _____

Cause and Effect Charts

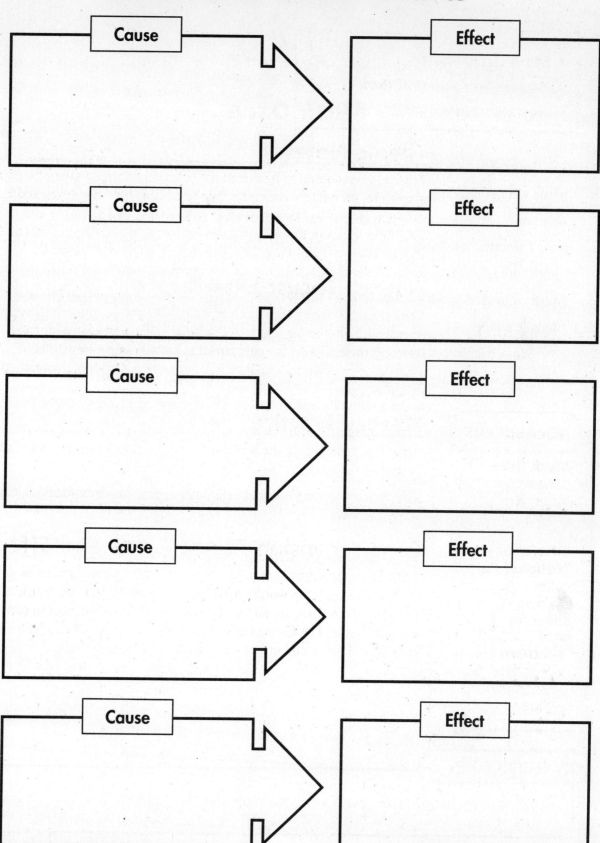

Lesson 5: Alaska
Connecting Reading 5–6, SV 9781419036446

Musk Oxen

	2

Musk oxen are back in Alaska! These heavy animals were once hunted until their | 16

herds were gone. Then people brought 34 wild musk oxen from Greenland in 1930. Today, | 31

thousands of these animals live in Alaska. Their **survival** is a success story. | 44

The name *musk oxen* means "animals with skin like a beard." Their dark brown hair | 59

almost drags on the ground. Under the dark hair is a very warm and soft wool called qiviut.* | 77

Musk oxen shed qiviut each year when **bitter** winter is past. Some people gather this wool | 93

to make clothes. | 96

Musk oxen's feet also help them live on the cold **tundra**. Do you know how? Their | 112

strong hooves can dig through snow to find food and break river ice to reach water. | 128

Adult musk oxen make a tight circle if wolves or a bear come near. This animal | 144

teamwork protects them from danger! | 149

* (KEE vee oot)

 **FLUENCY TIP**

Remember to change your voice for the question and exclamations.

Lesson 5: Alaska
Connecting Reading 5–6, SV 9781419036446

Musk Oxen Comprehension

Read each question. Darken the circle next to the correct answer.

1. Why were there no musk oxen in Alaska in 1930?

   Ⓐ Alaska is not a natural habitat for them.

   Ⓑ Hunters killed all of them.

   Ⓒ People in Greenland took them all.

   Ⓓ They all froze to death.

2. What does qiviut do for musk oxen?

   Ⓐ It protects them from the cold.

   Ⓑ It breaks through ice.

   Ⓒ It makes a beard.

   Ⓓ It makes clothes.

3. What breaks the ice so the musk oxen can get water?

   Ⓐ the qiviut

   Ⓑ the head

   Ⓒ the hooves

   Ⓓ the tail

4. How does making a circle keep musk oxen safe?

   Ⓐ The musk oxen can see from all directions.

   Ⓑ Dangerous animals won't go near a circle.

   Ⓒ The dangerous animals can't get through the beards.

   Ⓓ It keeps them warm in the cold winter.

Answer the question using complete sentences.

5. How are musk oxen suited to living in frozen areas of Alaska?

_____

_____

_____

    Connecting Reading 5–6, SV 9781419036446

Glacier Bay National Park

	4
Sometimes nature wipes an area clean. Then life starts over. This happened at	17
Glacier Bay.	19
Bitter ice rivers covered the area nearly 4,000 years ago. Then some of these **glaciers**	34
began melting around 1750. However, melting takes time at Glacier Bay!	45
Today, visitors travel by boats into the bay. On the bay's east side, they glide past	61
forests. The trees have had time to grow where the ice melted first. Next, visitors travel past	78
younger, smaller plants before they reach the melting glaciers.	89
Melting is NOT happening on the bay's west side. Ice from mountains is still slowly	104
moving into Glacier Bay. Large parts of these glaciers are hidden underwater. The tops	118
towering above water look like mountains of ice!	126

⚙️ **FLUENCY TIP**

Your reading should sound like you're talking, not flat.

Connecting Reading 5–6, SV 9781419036446

Glacier Bay National Park Comprehension

Read each question. Darken the circle next to the correct answer.

1. What is a glacier?

Ⓐ rocks

Ⓑ ice

Ⓒ trees

Ⓓ wind

2. What is the weather like most of the time in Glacier Bay?

Ⓐ hot

Ⓑ cold

Ⓒ windy

Ⓓ rainy

3. How do people visit Glacier Bay?

Ⓐ by car

Ⓑ by train

Ⓒ by sled

Ⓓ by boat

4. Where is the biggest part of each glacier?

Ⓐ above water

Ⓑ under the water

Ⓒ on land

Ⓓ buried deep in the land

Answer the question using complete sentences.

5. How did life start over in Glacier Bay?

_____

_____

_____

Northern Lights

2

19

31

47

60

68

82

97

113

126

128

A **stupendous** sky show can often be seen on a dark, clear night in Alaska. What is this natural show? It is called the northern lights, or an aurora.*

No two auroras are ever alike. An aurora might appear as a rippling curtain or stripes streaking downward. Sometimes an aurora looks like swirls of rising smoke. Viewers may see green, red, or purple in an aurora.

An aurora is not a weather event, though. In fact, this **phenomenon** actually occurs high above Earth's clouds. Tiny specks of matter flow out from Earth's magnetic North Pole and the sun. The gases **collide** when they meet, producing electricity. As a result, an aurora light is produced. Alaskans often experience this powerful and colorful display during their dark winters.

* (uh ROR uh)

⚙ FLUENCY TIP

Remember to read important words longer, louder, or with a different pitch of your voice.

Name _____ Date _____

Northern Lights Comprehension

Read each question. Darken the circle next to the correct answer.

1. What is another name for the northern lights?
   - Ⓐ Alaskan lights
   - Ⓑ skylights
   - Ⓒ aurora
   - Ⓓ colorful gases

2. Where does some of the matter come from?
   - Ⓐ clouds
   - Ⓑ North Pole
   - Ⓒ Earth
   - Ⓓ smoke

3. What happens when the matter and the gases hit each other?
   - Ⓐ They make a magnet.
   - Ⓑ They make clouds.
   - Ⓒ They make winter.
   - Ⓓ They make electricity.

4. When do people most often see the northern lights?
   - Ⓐ spring
   - Ⓑ summer
   - Ⓒ winter
   - Ⓓ fall

Answer the question using complete sentences.

5. Why might no two light shows be the same?

   _____

   _____

   _____

Lesson 5: Alaska
Connecting Reading 5–6, SV 9781419036446

Lesson 6: Change Is Good
Connecting Background

LEVELED TITLES

- *The Arctic Fox — 4.4*
- *The Anteater — 5.6*
- *The Polar Bear — 6.5*

Theme Notes

The land and weather change throughout the year in many places. Animals must adapt to the environment to be able to survive in it. Some migrate, or move away. Others have bodies that change. A third group rests during difficult conditions. In this lesson, readers will learn about how the arctic fox, anteater, and polar bear adapt during the year.

Fluency Focus: Expression

Fluent readers focus on expression as they read. It makes the selection more interesting and helps improve understanding. Sometimes, the reader needs to think about the purpose of a sentence before reading to decide which parts are important. Then the reader should use tone and rhythm to stress those words to emphasize meaning.

Fluency Practice

Write these sentences on the board: *Look at those geese flying overhead! Do you think they are heading south for the winter?*

Discuss the purpose of the punctuation. Invite volunteers to read the sentences fluently.

Comprehension Focus: Main Idea and Supporting Details

The main idea describes what the text is mostly about. Details tell more about the main idea. When authors don't state the main idea directly, readers have to find clues in the text to find it. The title, repeated words, and pictures often give clues. The graphic organizer on page 49 can help students identify the main idea and supporting details of their selections.

VOCABULARY

- *The Arctic Fox*
  adapted
  camouflages
  prey

- *The Anteater*
  species
  glands
  positioned

- *The Polar Bear*
  adaptations
  camouflage
  pursue

Main Idea and Supporting Details
Graphic Organizer

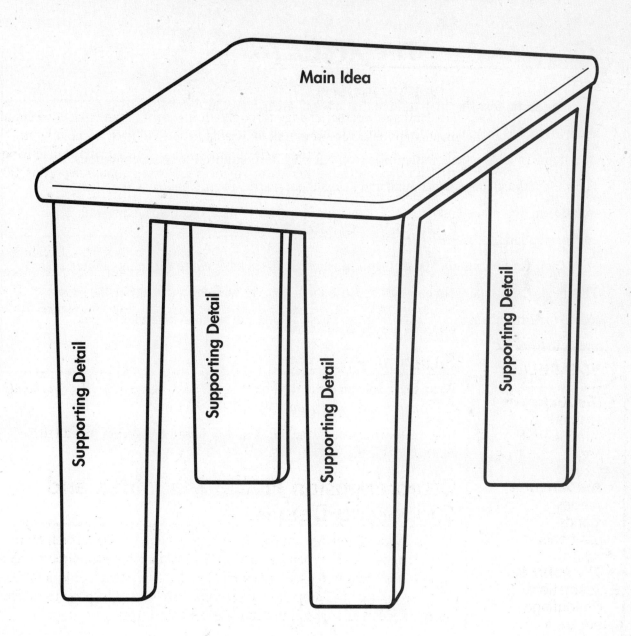

Main Idea

Supporting Detail

Supporting Detail

Supporting Detail

Supporting Detail

Connecting Reading 5–6, SV 9781419036446

Name _____ Date _____

The Arctic Fox

3
20
36
51
66
82
85
99
115
131
135

The arctic fox is a small animal that lives in areas near the Arctic Circle. It is about 20 inches long, not including its tail, and it weighs from 7 to 17 pounds.

It is very cold where arctic foxes live, but they have **adapted** to these conditions. Their long, thick fur protects them and keeps them warm. Their small ears keep them from losing too much body heat. Fur covering the soles of their feet helps them walk on freezing land.

Their fur also **camouflages** them. Most arctic foxes have white fur in the winter. This helps them hide from enemies because they blend in with the snow. After the snow melts, their fur changes to brown or gray. These changes in fur also help them sneak up on their **prey**.

⚙ FLUENCY TIP

To practice reading with expression, read the first paragraph to a partner. Remember to emphasize important words.

Name _____ Date _____

The Arctic Fox Comprehension

Read each question. Darken the circle next to the correct answer.

1. What does *adapt* mean?

Ⓐ the place where an animal lives

Ⓑ to blend in

Ⓒ to change so as to be able to survive

Ⓓ an animal that hunts another animal for food

2. How does the arctic fox get its name?

Ⓐ It lives in a cold place.

Ⓑ It lives near the Arctic Circle.

Ⓒ It hunts other arctic animals.

Ⓓ Its fur is white like snow.

3. How do the small ears of the arctic fox help it?

Ⓐ They do not lose much heat.

Ⓑ They help it hear well.

Ⓒ They help it hide.

Ⓓ They keep the animal from getting too hot.

4. What is the main idea of the article?

Ⓐ The arctic fox is a small animal.

Ⓑ The arctic fox is a hunter.

Ⓒ The arctic fox has a body that helps it stay safe.

Ⓓ The arctic fox lives in a very cold land.

Answer the question using complete sentences.

5. What is the land around the Arctic Circle like in the summer? Explain why you think as you do.

_____

_____

_____

Connecting Reading 5–6, SV 9781419036446

Name _____ Date _____

The Anteater

2
17
32
50
69
83
99
116
134

The anteater is a toothless animal that lives in tropical forests in Central and South America. One **species**, the giant anteater, grows over six feet in length, including its tail. This creature has a tube-shaped head with a long, thin snout. It uses its sharp sense of smell to track its food. The mouth is small, but the tongue can be up to 24 inches long. **Glands** produce sticky saliva on the tongue. The anteater uses its tongue to gather food.

An anteater walks with its front feet **positioned** sideways to protect its claws. It uses its claws to tear open insect nests and to defend itself. When in danger, the anteater perches on its back legs and tail, like a tripod. Then it uses its front legs to strike the enemy.

> ## ⚙ FLUENCY TIP
>
> When reading factual information, you can show expression by emphasizing words in each sentence. For example, in the first sentence, emphasize *toothless* and *tropical forests*.

www.harcourtschoolsupply.com

Lesson 6: Change Is Good
Connecting Reading 5–6, SV 9781419036446

The Anteater Comprehension

Read each question. Darken the circle next to the correct answer.

1. How does an anteater find its food?

Ⓐ sight

Ⓑ smell

Ⓒ taste

Ⓓ feel

2. How does a sticky tongue help an anteater?

Ⓐ Insects stick to it.

Ⓑ It makes insects taste better.

Ⓒ It strikes the insects.

Ⓓ It pokes the insects.

3. Why does an anteater get up on its hind legs?

Ⓐ Its front legs are free to strike an enemy.

Ⓑ It can reach insect nests.

Ⓒ It can move by hopping.

Ⓓ It can catch and hold food.

4. What is the main idea of the article?

Ⓐ The anteater has to eat insects because it does not have teeth.

Ⓑ The anteater likes to fight.

Ⓒ The anteater has body parts that help it live.

Ⓓ The anteater lives in the tropical forest.

Answer the question using complete sentences.

5. What are the claws of an anteater probably like? Explain why you think as you do.

_____

_____

_____

The Polar Bear

Polar bears have numerous **adaptations** that help them to be fantastic hunters. They have thick layers of fat beneath their skin and fur that protect them from very cold temperatures. This is necessary since polar bears roam wild in Alaska, Canada, Greenland, Russia, and on islands of the Arctic Ocean. Since they are often in snow, their white fur helps **camouflage** them from their prey.

Polar bears are great swimmers and good climbers. Polar bears can **pursue** their prey for long distances, and polar bears may be found many miles from land or ice. On land, they can run for short distances at speeds of up to 35 miles per hour.

Polar bears have a very good sense of smell, which helps them detect food as much as ten miles away. They can also smell prey that is covered by thick layers of snow or ice.

Polar bear feet have also adapted to the harsh extremes of ice and cold. The soles of a polar bear's feet are covered with hair to protect them from the cold and help the bear move across ice.

3
15
32
45
62
68
82
99
114
131
149
167
185
187

⚙ FLUENCY TIP

Use your voice to emphasize words in this article. For example, in the first sentence of the last paragraph, emphasize *feet*, *harsh*, and *cold*.

Name _____ Date _____

The Polar Bear Comprehension

Read each question. Darken the circle next to the correct answer.

1. Which does NOT help polar bears in the cold?

Ⓐ layers of fat

Ⓑ thick fur

Ⓒ good sense of smell

Ⓓ hair on their feet

2. How does white fur help the polar bear?

Ⓐ The prey cannot see it coming.

Ⓑ The bear can swim faster.

Ⓒ The bear can stay warmer.

Ⓓ The bear can smell better.

3. Where might you find a polar bear in the wild?

Ⓐ Alaska

Ⓑ Mexico

Ⓒ Poland

Ⓓ Spain

4. Which sentence from the article tells the main idea?

Ⓐ *Polar bears have numerous adaptations that help them to be fantastic hunters.*

Ⓑ *On land, they can run for short distances at speeds of up to 35 miles per hour.*

Ⓒ *Polar bear feet have also adapted to the harsh extremes of ice and cold.*

Ⓓ *Polar bears are great swimmers and good climbers.*

Answer the question using complete sentences.

5. Why is the polar bear a good hunter?

_____

_____

_____

Lesson 6: Change Is Good
Connecting Reading 5–6, SV 9781419036446

Lesson 7: Who's Your Mummy?

Connecting Background

Theme Notes

The Pyramids are a well-known tourist attraction in Egypt. They were the burial sites for wealthy ancient Egyptians. They were often filled with priceless gems, statues, and of course, mummies. This lesson focuses on the mysteries of the Pyramids and mummies, as well as the boy ruler King Tut.

Fluency Focus: Phrasing

To read fluently, readers need to read sentences in chunks, or phrases, instead of stopping after each word. This makes the text sound smoother and can help improve understanding. Often punctuation helps a reader phrase correctly. However, sometimes the reader needs to figure out the phrasing. The key is grouping words that look and sound like they go together.

Fluency Practice

Write this sentence on the board: *Scientists like to dig in the sand near pyramids looking for artifacts from ancient life.*

Have students write the sentence and draw a slash between each natural-sounding phrase. Then encourage them to practice reading the sentence fluently.

VOCABULARY

- **Mummy**
  creepy
  ancient
  entire

- **The Pyramids**
  pharaohs
  tomb
  suffered

- **King Tut**
  tombs
  archaeologists
  hieroglyphic

Comprehension Focus: Asking Questions

Good readers pause to ask questions. Then they search for the answers. Asking questions helps them focus on what they are reading. It helps them clarify when something in the text seems confusing. It also helps them think more deeply about what they are reading. Have students use the Nonfiction Questions and Answers Chart on page 57 to help them track questions as they read.

www.harcourtschoolsupply.com
© Harcourt Achieve Inc. All rights reserved.

56

Lesson 7: Who's Your Mummy?
Connecting Reading 5–6, SV 9781419036446

Name _____ Date _____

Nonfiction Questions and Answers Chart

Before Reading		During Reading	After Reading
What do I know about this topic?	What do I want to find out about this topic?	What did I learn?	What new questions do I have?

Lesson 7: Who's Your Mummy?
Connecting Reading 5–6, SV 9781419036446

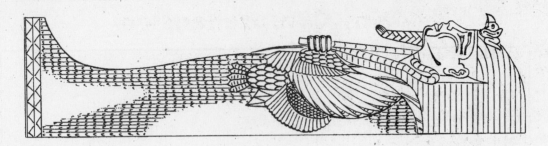

Mummy

1
13
28
41
55
71
90
107
127
142
155
166

Mummies aren't just something from **creepy** science fiction movies. They are actually people who lived long ago. These people were often wealthy. They wanted their bodies kept in good condition. They believed they needed their bodies for life after death.

Ancient Egyptians learned ways to keep the bodies of the dead in good condition. Here is how the Egyptians made mummies. First, they removed all the organs from the dead body. They put the organs in jars. Then, they covered the **entire** body in salt and let it dry for one month. Next, they wrapped the body in linen. They put charms and jewels in the layers of the cloth. In the next step, the body was wrapped in a sheet. The Book of the Dead was also placed in the sheet. Finally, workers coated the sheet with wax and perfume.

Today scientists use powerful X-rays to view a mummy's skeleton and the objects buried with it. X-rays help scientists answer questions about these people.

⚙ FLUENCY TIP

To practice phrasing, rewrite the first paragraph. Draw a slash mark (/) after each phrase. For example: "In the past / scientists unwrapped mummies / to study them."

www.harcourtschoolsupply.com
© Harcourt Achieve Inc. All rights reserved.

58

Lesson 7: Who's Your Mummy?
Connecting Reading 5–6, SV 9781419036446

Name _____ Date _____

Mummy Comprehension

Read each question. Darken the circle next to the correct answer.

1. Why did people make mummies?

   Ⓐ The dead would need their body in the next life.

   Ⓑ The relatives wanted to visit the bodies later.

   Ⓒ There was no place to bury people.

   Ⓓ The mummies were symbols of power.

2. Where are mummies found?

   Ⓐ in England

   Ⓑ in Egypt

   Ⓒ in France

   Ⓓ in Canada

3. What did the people do first to make a mummy?

   Ⓐ covered the body in salt

   Ⓑ put charms on the body

   Ⓒ took out the organs

   Ⓓ wrapped the body in a sheet

4. How do we learn about mummies today?

   Ⓐ The Book of the Dead tells about mummies.

   Ⓑ Ancient Egyptians drew pictures.

   Ⓒ The wealthy people left letters.

   Ⓓ Scientists use X-rays to look inside.

Answer the question using complete sentences.

5. What supplies were needed to wrap a mummy?

   _____

   _____

   _____

The Pyramids

| | 2 |

To the ancient Egyptians, the **pharaohs** were not only kings—they were gods. The | 16

people believed that a pharaoh lived with the gods after he died. Because of this belief, the | 33

pharaoh's body had to be protected for its next life. Only the biggest, most fantastic **tomb** | 49

would do. As a result, Egyptians built pyramids. | 57

Many people think the Giza Pyramids are the finest in the world. They are still | 72

standing after 4,500 years! Workers built the Pyramids with stone blocks. The blocks are | 86

heavier than minivans. Scientists do not know how the builders constructed the Pyramids. | 99

It is one of the mysteries of ancient Egypt. | 108

The Pyramids have **suffered** much damage over the years. Builders have taken the | 121

limestone from the outside to build a nearby city. Robbers have stripped the tombs of their | 137

treasures. Although they have lost some of their glory, the Pyramids remain true wonders | 151

of the world. | 154

⚙️ FLUENCY TIP

Look at the second sentence. Reread it to a partner, pausing after *believed* and *gods*.

Lesson 7: Who's Your Mummy?
Connecting Reading 5–6, SV 9781419036446

Name _____ Date _____

The Pyramids **Comprehension**

Read each question. Darken the circle next to the correct answer.

1. What did the ancient Egyptians believe about their kings?

Ⓐ They were scientists.

Ⓑ They had to live in a pyramid.

Ⓒ They were gods.

Ⓓ They were robbers.

2. What is a pyramid?

Ⓐ a tomb

Ⓑ a museum

Ⓒ a workshop

Ⓓ a city

3. Why are the Pyramids a mystery?

Ⓐ No one knows what kind of stone was used.

Ⓑ Scientists are not sure how they were built.

Ⓒ People don't know how old they are.

Ⓓ No one knows who built them.

4. How did builders hurt the Pyramids?

Ⓐ They used some of the stones in other buildings.

Ⓑ They moved the Pyramids to make room for new buildings.

Ⓒ They stored minivans in them.

Ⓓ They stole the treasures.

Answer the question using complete sentences.

5. Why are the Pyramids considered to be a wonder of the world?

_____

_____

_____

Connecting Reading 5–6, SV 9781419036446

King Tut

	2
For over 3,000 years, kings and queens called pharaohs ruled ancient Egypt. They were	16
considered god-like. The pharaoh and his family had the finest linens and jewels. They lived	31
in luxury. When they died, the pharaohs were buried with these riches.	43

For over 3,000 years, kings and queens called pharaohs ruled ancient Egypt. They were considered god-like. The pharaoh and his family had the finest linens and jewels. They lived in luxury. When they died, the pharaohs were buried with these riches.

Knowing this, robbers broke into their **tombs** to steal the riches. However, one pharaoh's tomb, that of King Tutankhamen, was spared. In 1922, **archaeologists** opened Tut's tomb. They were amazed by the treasures inside. Tut wore a spectacular gold mask. The Egyptians had buried many priceless pieces of jewelry with him as well. The tomb contained shrines of gold covered with **hieroglyphic** text. It also held furniture, statues, clothes, weapons, and a chariot. You can view some of Tut's treasures online at the Egyptian Museum's Web site.

Known as the boy king, Tutankhamen ruled from age nine until about eighteen. Recent evidence suggests that Tut died from an infection resulting from a broken leg. Before this discovery, many thought he had been murdered.

56
68
83
98
111
127
130
144
159
166

⚙️ **FLUENCY TIP**

The second sentence of the second paragraph may be difficult. Reread it to a partner, pausing after each comma for proper phrasing.

Connecting Reading 5–6, SV 9781419036446

King Tut Comprehension

Read each question. Darken the circle next to the correct answer.

1. Who ruled ancient Egypt?

Ⓐ emperors

Ⓑ priests

Ⓒ pharaohs

Ⓓ generals

2. Which of these would an archaeologist most like to find?

Ⓐ a painting

Ⓑ a tomb

Ⓒ a microwave

Ⓓ a wooden wagon

3. What was so amazing about King Tut's tomb?

Ⓐ No one found it.

Ⓑ It had a mummy.

Ⓒ It was filled with treasures.

Ⓓ King Tut was not in it.

4. How did King Tut die?

Ⓐ He was murdered.

Ⓑ He got sick from eating bad food.

Ⓒ He had an infection.

Ⓓ He had a heart attack.

Answer the question using complete sentences.

5. What might scientists learn by looking at the treasures buried with King Tut?

_____

_____

_____

Lesson 8: Water, Water, Everywhere
Connecting Background

LEVELED TITLES

- *A River of Ice* — 4.6
- *Oceans, Oceans, Everywhere* — 6.1
- *The Lifeline of the Southwest* — 6.8

Theme Notes

Water is everywhere. In fact, over 71 percent of Earth's surface is water. Most often, people think of water as a liquid that people drink, play in, and clean with. But in this lesson, readers find out other reasons water is so important when they read about oceans, rivers, and glaciers.

Fluency Focus: Word Accuracy

Fluent readers read accurately. They put sounds and word parts together to read more smoothly. When coming to an unfamiliar word, readers should look for smaller word parts and blend the sounds to make the word. Then they should practice the word until they can say it smoothly and naturally.

Fluency Practice

Write this sentence on the board: *Water is one of the most powerful forces on Earth and can cause much destruction.*

Circle *powerful* and *destruction*. Model how to break each word into parts, sound them out, and then blend the parts together. Have partners practice reading the sentence fluently.

Comprehension Focus: Making Connections

Making connections means that readers think about what they already know about a given topic. They can think about a personal experience or another source they have read. By making a connection, readers relate the text to the previous information, which results in a deeper understanding of the topic. The Text Connections Web on page 65 can help students make the connection to the topics of the lesson.

VOCABULARY

- *A River of Ice*
  eventually
  layers
  eternity

- *Oceans, Oceans, Everywhere*
  dissolve
  destruction
  preserve

- *The Lifeline of the Southwest*
  reddish
  surging
  churning

Name _____ Date _____

Text Connections Web

Feelings	People	Personal Experiences	Pictures	Places	Other Books

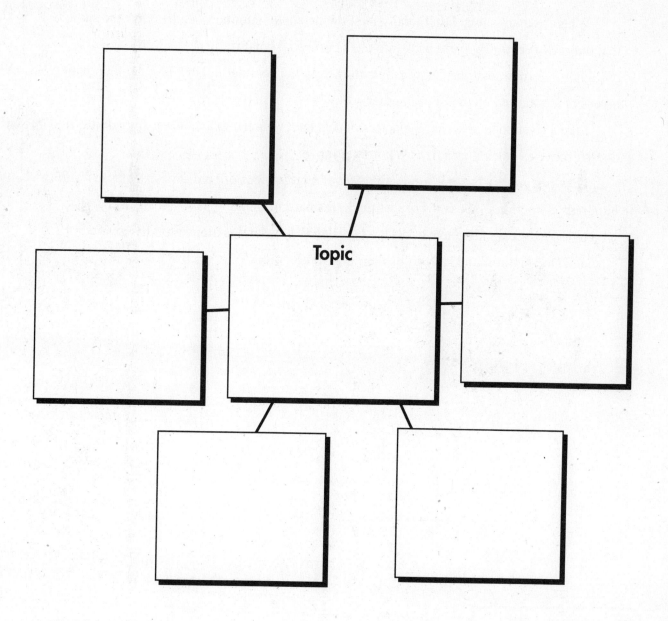

Name _____   Date _____

A River of Ice

4

What if winter snow didn't totally melt by the end of summer? And what if the snow
that did melt **eventually** froze back into ice again? And what if the next several winters
brought more snow, and that snow didn't all melt in the summer either? You'd end up with
layers of ice stacked on top of each other.

21
37
54
63

Like a river collects water, a glacier collects ice. A glacier is actually a river of ice. It
doesn't move as quickly as a river, but it does move.

81
92

Now imagine a glacier big enough to cover a large piece of land. These "ice caps" are
hundreds, sometimes thousands of feet thick. It's hard to imagine, isn't it? But ask anyone
who lives in Greenland—the world's largest island! This land is almost totally covered in
glaciers. Do you think the ice will be there for all **eternity**?

109
124
139
151

 **FLUENCY TIP**

Remember to break larger words into smaller parts.

Lesson 8: Water, Water, Everywhere
Connecting Reading 5–6, SV 9781419036446

Name _____ Date _____

A River of Ice Comprehension

Read each question. Darken the circle next to the correct answer.

1. How is a glacier made?

Ⓐ A river freezes and never melts.

Ⓑ Snow piles on a mountain in a year.

Ⓒ Water freezes and then melts in the spring.

Ⓓ Layers of snow and ice stack up year after year.

2. How is a river like a glacier?

Ⓐ They both have moving water.

Ⓑ They both move.

Ⓒ They both start in the mountains.

Ⓓ They both are icy.

3. What is the most common weather in Greenland?

Ⓐ cold

Ⓑ hot

Ⓒ rainy

Ⓓ warm

4. What is *eternity*?

Ⓐ feeling helpless

Ⓑ a cold place

Ⓒ forever

Ⓓ quick

Answer the question using complete sentences.

5. Do you think the ice caps might ever melt? Why or why not?

_____

_____

_____

Lesson 8: Water, Water, Everywhere
Connecting Reading 5–6, SV 9781419036446

Oceans, Oceans, Everywhere

3

16
33
45
59
73
88
107
111
128
142
158
174
178

Imagine that you're swimming in the Atlantic Ocean and someone else is swimming in the Indian Ocean. Can you believe that you both are swimming in the same water? That's right! Even though the oceans have different names, they are all connected.

Here's another fact—oceans are salty. But you know that. As rivers and streams flow toward the oceans, they **dissolve** minerals on land. The running water carries these dissolved minerals to the ocean. The most abundant dissolved mineral is salt. But here is the interesting part. If you took all the salt out of the oceans, the mineral would be five feet deep all over Earth!

Out of all the planets in our solar system, Earth has the most water. Water covers about 71 percent of Earth's surface. Our oceans are important to our environment. Many people work to prevent the **destruction** of the oceans. Presently, there is a concern that the oceans are being over-fished, and raw sewage is often dumped into them. Find out ways you can help **preserve** this resource!

⚙ FLUENCY TIP

Find the words that have an *-ing* ending. Break those words into smaller parts so they are easier to read. Here is an example: *interest-ing*.

Name _____ Date _____

Oceans, Oceans, Everywhere Comprehension

Read each question. Darken the circle next to the correct answer.

1. How do scientists know that the oceans are all connected?

   Ⓐ The same mountains are underneath them.

   Ⓑ No land separates the water.

   Ⓒ The same fish swim all over.

   Ⓓ The oceans have the same current.

2. Why is the ocean salty?

   Ⓐ The waste from fish mixes with the water to make salt.

   Ⓑ Rivers and streams carry dissolved salt to the ocean.

   Ⓒ Swimming in it stirs up the salt.

   Ⓓ Raw sewage running into the ocean is salty.

3. How much of Earth is covered in water?

   Ⓐ 5 percent

   Ⓑ 17 percent

   Ⓒ 90 percent

   Ⓓ 71 percent

4. What is one problem the oceans face today?

   Ⓐ Too many fish are being caught.

   Ⓑ There is too much salt in them.

   Ⓒ Salty things are dissolving in them.

   Ⓓ People are concerned about the damage to them.

Answer the question using complete sentences.

5. What can you do to help preserve the oceans?

   _____

   _____

   _____

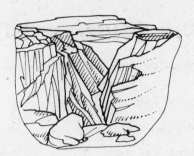

The Lifeline of the Southwest

What's 1,450 miles long, touches seven states, and serves as a boundary between parts of the United States and Mexico? If you guessed the Colorado River, you're right.

Explorers from Europe discovered the river in the early 1500s. Native American farmers were using it to water their crops. It wasn't until 1776 that the river got its name. *Colorado* means "**reddish** color" in Spanish.

The Colorado River is certainly important for its water. It is also important because it shapes the land it flows across. Its **surging** water and **churning** sand cut valleys into hard rock. Some cuts were very deep. How deep? The biggest valley is world famous. It's known as the Grand Canyon!

5
18
33
45
63
69
83
99
115
120

⚙ FLUENCY TIP

Look for ways to break a word into parts to make it easier to read.

The Lifeline of the Southwest Comprehension

Read each question. Darken the circle next to the correct answer.

1. Which is a fact about the Colorado River?

Ⓐ It runs through South Carolina.

Ⓑ It is a boundary between Canada and the United States.

Ⓒ It is more than 2,000 miles long.

Ⓓ It touches seven states.

2. Who named the river?

Ⓐ the English

Ⓑ the Native Americans

Ⓒ the Spanish

Ⓓ the French

3. How do you know that water is powerful?

Ⓐ It is loud when it flows.

Ⓑ It grows crops.

Ⓒ It can flow a long way.

Ⓓ It cuts through rocks.

4. What famous place was formed by water?

Ⓐ Mexico

Ⓑ Europe

Ⓒ the Grand Canyon

Ⓓ the Rocky Mountains

Answer the question using complete sentences.

5. How do you think the Colorado River got its name?

_____

_____

_____

Connecting Reading 5–6, SV 9781419036446

Lesson 9: Presidents Unite
Connecting Background

LEVELED TITLES

- *Teddy Bear Roosevelt* — 4.6
- *Lincoln Goes to "Blab" School* — 6.0
- *George Washington's Teeth* — 6.9

Theme Notes

The presidents of the United States have a very important job. Some of their responsibilities include enforcing federal laws, commanding the armed forces, making the nation's budget, and directing national security. They are often in the spotlight, so they have little privacy. There are many interesting, personal facts about past presidents, including George Washington, Abraham Lincoln, and Theodore Roosevelt.

Fluency Focus: Punctuation

Fluent readers know what punctuation is and what it stands for. They know to change the way they read based on the punctuation. They look for punctuation instead of skipping the marks and racing forward. Fluent readers stop at periods and pause at commas. They use a questioning voice for question marks and excitement at exclamation points.

VOCABULARY

- *Teddy Bear Roosevelt*
  nickname
  toymakers
  comfort

- *Lincoln Goes to "Blab" School*
  admired
  nicknamed
  pastimes

- *George Washington's Teeth*
  excruciating
  appearance
  peculiar

Fluency Practice

Write these sentences on the board: *"Hurry up!" he shouted. "Don't you know the president is about to get off the jet?"*

Point out the punctuation. Then have partners take turns reading the sentences with proper expression.

Comprehension Focus: Summarizing

When readers summarize, they tell the most important parts in a selection. The summary often includes the answers to *who, what, where, when, why,* and *how.* This skill is important, so a reader should periodically stop and check his or her understanding. Students can use the Summarizing Chart on page 73 to summarize the selections.

Name _____ Date _____

Summarizing Chart

	Summary
Who? _____	_____
_____	_____
What? _____	_____
_____	_____
Where? _____	_____
_____	_____
When? _____	_____
_____	_____
Why? _____	_____
_____	_____
How? _____	_____
_____	_____

Lesson 9: Presidents Unite
Connecting Reading 5–6, SV 9781419036446

Teddy Bear Roosevelt

	3

When you see a teddy bear, do you think about a president? Well, you will now!   19

Theodore Roosevelt was president from 1901 to 1909. His **nickname** was Teddy. Teddy   32

loved nature, especially animals.   36

    One day, Teddy was out enjoying nature. He saw a bear cub tied to a tree. A hunter had   55

tied it there. Bear hunting was a favorite sport of some people, but Teddy didn't think a cub   73

should be killed. So he let the cub go free.   83

    Many people heard this story and were touched by it. Two **toymakers** made a special   98

toy bear that they called a "Teddy bear." Many people wanted a teddy bear. The teddy bear   115

became a symbol of **comfort**. It is now one of America's favorite toys.   128

 **FLUENCY TIP**

Take a breath at each period, or you might run out of air in the wrong place!

www.harcourtschoolsupply.com
74
Lesson 9: Presidents Unite
Connecting Reading 5–6, SV 9781419036446

Teddy Bear Roosevelt Comprehension

Read each question. Darken the circle next to the correct answer.

1. What is this story mostly about?

Ⓐ the reason the teddy bear was created

Ⓑ the job of a president

Ⓒ the life of President Teddy Roosevelt

Ⓓ making teddy bears

2. According to the article, what did Teddy Roosevelt like to do?

Ⓐ hunt bears

Ⓑ go out in nature

Ⓒ play with teddy bears

Ⓓ talk with people

3. Why did the toymakers make a bear?

Ⓐ to remember the story about the president

Ⓑ to make something kids would like

Ⓒ to replace the one the hunter lost

Ⓓ to thank the president

4. Why is the teddy bear a favorite toy?

Ⓐ It helps people remember a president.

Ⓑ It looks like a real bear.

Ⓒ All hunters can have one.

Ⓓ It is soft and cute.

Answer the question using complete sentences.

5. What can you tell about President Teddy Roosevelt from this story? Explain.

_____

_____

_____

Lincoln Goes to "Blab" School

	5

Abraham Lincoln is one of the most **admired** presidents of the United States. He was | 20
born in Kentucky in 1809. At that time, many children learned to read at home. In areas | 37
where several families lived together, the parents might hire a teacher. The teacher taught | 51
children of all ages in a small, one-room schoolhouse. | 60

In the schoolhouse, children often learned to read by reading out loud. This helped | 74
the teacher hear how everyone was progressing. Imagine the sound of everyone reading | 87
aloud at once—blab, blab, blab. Soon these schools were **nicknamed** "blab" schools. | 100

Abraham Lincoln went to a blab school. In fact, he read aloud so much that | 115
he frequently did it as an adult. Even when he was president, people could hear him | 131
reading aloud. | 133

Reading and writing were among Abraham Lincoln's favorite **pastimes**. These | 143
skills helped him become a respected speaker. People say that he was the best writer and | 159
speechmaker of all the presidents. | 164

 **FLUENCY TIP**

A long dash is a punctuation mark that signals you to pause briefly.

Lincoln Goes to "Blab" School Comprehension

Read each question. Darken the circle next to the correct answer.

1. Why did children of all ages learn in one-room schoolhouses a long time ago?

Ⓐ They all did the same work.

Ⓑ Children didn't go to school for very long.

Ⓒ They went to school only in the summer.

Ⓓ There was only one teacher.

2. What word best describes a one-room schoolhouse?

Ⓐ noisy

Ⓑ quiet

Ⓒ cheerful

Ⓓ confusing

3. What does *blab* mean?

Ⓐ a big spot

Ⓑ lots of talking

Ⓒ reading books

Ⓓ doing work

4. How could reading out loud help someone give a speech?

Ⓐ The person is used to talking in front of people.

Ⓑ The person practices reading with expression.

Ⓒ The person learns to yell.

Ⓓ The person learns to write better.

Answer the question using complete sentences.

5. How can reading aloud help you become a better reader?

_____

_____

_____

Name _____ Date _____

George Washington's Teeth

Do you know which president had only one tooth when he took office? Did you guess 19
George Washington? 21

Back in George Washington's time, people didn't know the importance of dental care. 34
This often resulted in rotten teeth. The diseased teeth were generally left in the mouth 49
until they fell out. Imagine the **excruciating** pain those people experienced! If people were 63
lucky enough to visit a dentist, he would pull out the tooth to halt the pain. 79

Eventually, George needed a set of false teeth to improve his **appearance**. You may 93
have heard that George had wooden teeth, but that isn't true. George's false teeth were made 109
from original cow and hippo teeth. 115

Unfortunately, the false teeth were too big for George's mouth and caused him lots of 130
pain. Moreover, they gave him a **peculiar** smile. In fact, if you view any portrait of George, 147
you will notice that his lips are pressed tightly together to hide his teeth. People thought 163
George was just being serious, but he was actually hiding his funny-looking teeth! 176

⚙ FLUENCY TIP

Look ahead for end punctuation. You need to be ready to change your voice for an exclamation or question.

Connecting Reading 5–6, SV 9781419036446

George Washington's Teeth Comprehension

Read each question. Darken the circle next to the correct answer.

1. Why did teeth often fall out long ago?

   Ⓐ People did not know how to care for teeth.

   Ⓑ There were no dentists.

   Ⓒ People ate unhealthy foods.

   Ⓓ Baby teeth fell out, and adult teeth never grew.

2. How could people stop the pain?

   Ⓐ pull out the teeth

   Ⓑ stop eating

   Ⓒ use wooden teeth

   Ⓓ keep their lips closed

3. What were Washington's teeth made of?

   Ⓐ wood

   Ⓑ apples

   Ⓒ animal teeth

   Ⓓ human teeth

4. What did Washington probably think about his teeth?

   Ⓐ They looked good.

   Ⓑ They felt comfortable.

   Ⓒ They were not good.

   Ⓓ They tickled.

Answer the question using complete sentences.

5. What lesson could someone learn from this article?

   _____

   _____

   _____

Lesson 10: Fight for the Right
Connecting Background

LEVELED TITLES

- *Evangeline Booth* — 4.8
- *Lewis Hine* — 6.1
- *Jane Addams* — 7.0

Theme Notes

Social reformers are people who work to change things in society that they see are wrong. They are often common people who sometimes become famous for their efforts. Many of the social reformers of the past were everyday people who worked to improve the life of others. This lesson focuses on the lives of Evangeline Booth, Lewis Hine, and Jane Addams.

Fluency Focus: Word Accuracy

To read fluently, readers need to know the words. Fluent readers read all the words with accuracy. They learn how to pronounce the words, and they learn what the words mean. In articles about people and places, it is especially important to correctly pronounce the proper nouns.

Fluency Practice

Write this sentence on the board: *Jane Addams was a social reformer who was born in Cedarville, Illinois.*

Have students circle the proper nouns and rehearse them to develop automaticity. Then invite partners to take turns reading the sentence.

Comprehension Focus: Sequence

Biographies tell about a person's life. The events are often recounted in sequence. Sequence is the order in which events happen. Clue words can help a reader understand the sequence of life events. Words like *first, next, last,* and *finally* tell about sequence. Dates are also clues that tell time sequence. The Sequence Chain on page 81 can help students understand the order of events in each biography.

VOCABULARY

- *Evangeline Booth*
  organization
  passion
  pretended

- *Lewis Hine*
  passion
  involved
  employers

- *Jane Addams*
  organize
  involved
  autobiography

Name _____ Date _____

Sequence Chain

Title _____

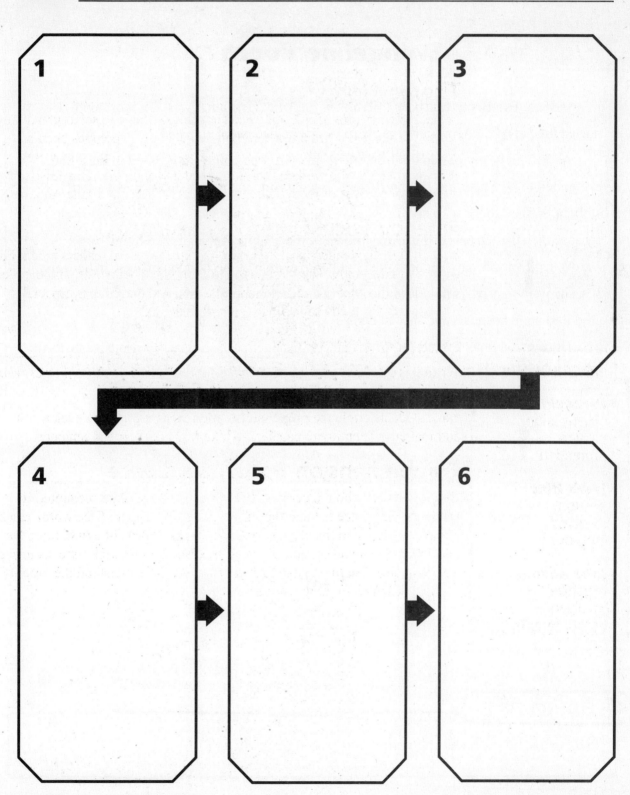

Evangeline Booth

2

In 1865, Eva Booth was born in London, England. Her father was William Booth. He started the Salvation Army, an **organization** that helped people in need.

17
28

As Eva grew, her **passion** to help others grew. At one point, she dressed in rags. She **pretended** to be a poor girl selling flowers. Beggars and the poor thought Eva was one of them, so they spoke with her. They told Eva all of their problems. She was able to help because they trusted her. Eva became known as the "White Angel of the Slums."

45
61
80
94

When Eva was only 23, her father put her in charge of the London offices. In her early 30s, she went to New York to lead the American movement. She raised a lot of money and used it to build hospitals and special homes.

112
130
138

During this time, Eva changed her name to Evangeline. She chose a serious name to fit the serious work she did.

154
159

⚙ FLUENCY TIP

Practice pronouncing all the names and places correctly.

www.harcourtschoolsupply.com
82
Lesson 10: **Fight for the Right**
Connecting Reading 5–6, SV 9781419036446

Evangeline Booth Comprehension

Read each question. Darken the circle next to the correct answer.

1. Where did the Salvation Army begin?

Ⓐ Chicago, Illinois

Ⓑ London, England

Ⓒ New York, New York

Ⓓ Paris, France

2. What was the main purpose of the Salvation Army?

Ⓐ to help women

Ⓑ to build hospitals

Ⓒ to help those in need

Ⓓ to find work for people

3. What did Eva do after heading up the London Salvation Army offices?

Ⓐ She started the Salvation Army in the United States.

Ⓑ She changed her last name.

Ⓒ She dressed in rags.

Ⓓ She sold flowers.

4. Why did Eva change her name?

Ⓐ She wanted an adult name.

Ⓑ She needed a new name in her new home.

Ⓒ Someone already had the name Eva at the Salvation Army.

Ⓓ She wanted a serious name.

Answer the question using complete sentences.

5. Why would dressing in rags change how people think?

_____

_____

_____

Lewis Hine

	2

In 1911, two million children were working in the United States. They worked in | 16
mines where they had to dig or factories where things were made. Many worked twelve | 31
hours a day for very low pay. Some people wanted to stop the practice that they called | 48
"child slavery." One of these people was Lewis Hine. | 57

In the early 1900s, Lewis Hine was a teacher in New York City. He began to learn | 74
photography and how to take pictures. What started as a hobby soon became a **passion**. | 89
Lewis learned the power of pictures. He took photographs of families with little money and | 104
discovered the horrible situation of many children. He became **involved** with groups trying | 117
to improve their working conditions. Lewis traveled across the country taking photographs | 129
of kids hard at work. | 134

Employers didn't want Lewis taking photographs. They did not let him enter the | 147
buildings or mines. To get inside, Lewis pretended to be a fire safety inspector. Other times | 163
he said he needed to take pictures of the machines. | 173

Many people didn't believe children were being treated poorly. Lewis's pictures opened | 185
their eyes. His pictures helped get new laws passed that would protect children. | 198

⚙ FLUENCY TIP

Make sure you read all the words. Do not skip words. If there is a word you are unsure about, look it up.

Name _____ Date _____

Lewis Hine Comprehension

Read each question. Darken the circle next to the correct answer.

1. Why were children working in the 1900s?

Ⓐ They wanted money to buy games.

Ⓑ They earned money to help their families.

Ⓒ They liked to work with machines.

Ⓓ Rich people made them work.

2. What did Lewis do while teaching?

Ⓐ learned photography

Ⓑ worked in a factory

Ⓒ took pictures of families

Ⓓ inspected factories

3. Why didn't owners want Lewis to take pictures inside factories?

Ⓐ He would see old machines.

Ⓑ He would see secret ways factories made things.

Ⓒ He would see children working in bad conditions.

Ⓓ He would see how much money the owners made.

4. What happened after people saw Lewis's pictures?

Ⓐ People made laws about children working in factories.

Ⓑ The owners were happy to help children.

Ⓒ The children in the pictures were fired.

Ⓓ The factories were forced to close.

Answer the question using complete sentences.

5. What picture have you seen that affected the way you think? Describe the picture and your feelings.

_____

_____

_____

Lesson 10: Fight for the Right
Connecting Reading 5–6, SV 9781419036446

Jane Addams

	2

Jane Addams was born in 1860 in Illinois. When she was two, her mother died. Jane's | 18

father encouraged her to work hard and to be honest and generous. Jane listened to her | 34

father. She spent her life working hard to help poor people. | 45

While on a tour of England, Jane saw a settlement house in the slums of London. The | 62

settlement house was a place that provided community services to poor people in a city | 77

neighborhood. Jane thought it was an excellent idea and would be a valuable service in the | 93

United States. She decided to **organize** a settlement house in Chicago. | 104

Jane founded her settlement house, called Hull House, in 1889. Within a few years, | 118

Hull House offered medical care, child care, and legal aid. It provided classes for immigrants | 133

so they could learn English as well as the necessary work skills to help them find jobs. It | 151

also gave the poor an opportunity to learn music, art, and drama. | 163

Jane saw another need in her community and turned her energies to a new cause. The | 179

factories required that their workers—men, women, and children—work long hours for low | 193

pay. Jane quickly became **involved** in improving the working conditions in factories. Some | 206

businessmen hinted that they would make a generous donation to Hull House if Jane gave up | 222

this effort. Jane replied that she would rather sing over the ruins of Hull House than give up. | 240

Later in life, Jane wrote her **autobiography**, which she titled *Twenty Years at* | 253

Hull House. | 255

⚙ FLUENCY TIP

Don't let an unusual word like *Hull* trick you. Be sure to read *Hull*, not *Hall* or *Hill*.

Lesson 10: Fight for the Right
Connecting Reading 5–6, SV 9781419036446

Jane Addams Comprehension

Read each question. Darken the circle next to the correct answer.

1. Who shaped Jane's life the most?

Ⓐ her mother

Ⓑ her father

Ⓒ businessmen

Ⓓ doctors

2. What did a settlement house do?

Ⓐ gave medical care, child care, and classes

Ⓑ helped factories find workers

Ⓒ gave Addams money

Ⓓ served food

3. What did Addams do after starting Hull House?

Ⓐ She worked with businessmen to make factories safer.

Ⓑ She organized factory workers for a protest.

Ⓒ She started a new settlement house.

Ⓓ She helped poor factory workers.

4. Why did the businessmen want to give Addams money?

Ⓐ They were bribing Addams to keep her away.

Ⓑ They were asking for her help.

Ⓒ They were being generous to help her.

Ⓓ The money was to go to the poor.

Answer the question using complete sentences.

5. Who has shaped your life? Explain.

_____

_____

_____

www.harcourtschoolsupply.com
87
Lesson 10: Fight for the Right
Connecting Reading 5–6, SV 9781419036446

Lesson 11: It's a Capital Idea!

Connecting Background

LEVELED TITLES

- *Is the White House a Zoo?* — 5.0
- *The Capitol Building* — 6.2
- *Arlington Heroes* — 7.2

Theme Notes

Washington, D.C., is the capital of the United States. It is the home of the president of the United States and the location for all the major offices of the federal government. Moreover, it represents freedom and equality for all the world to see. The readings in this lesson cover some interesting topics relating to the capital city—White House pets, the Capitol Building, and Arlington National Cemetery.

Fluency Focus: Phrasing

Phrasing is an important aspect of fluent reading. When reading word-for-word, readers may not understand the meaning of a sentence. Focusing on punctuation can help a reader phrase properly. Chunking words into phrases that make sense can also help improve meaning. If a sentence doesn't make sense, readers should try chunking it differently.

Fluency Practice

Write this sentence on the board: *The U.S. White House has 132 rooms, including 3 kitchens and 32 bathrooms.*

Challenge partners to read the sentence several times, chunking it differently each time. Have them choose the way that sounds like natural speech and rehearse it.

Comprehension Focus: Monitoring Comprehension

When monitoring comprehension, readers check to make sure they understand the text. Good readers realize when they do not understand and then use strategies to help themselves, including asking for help or looking for information in the paragraph. Students can use the Monitoring Comprehension Chart on page 89 to record sentences and words they don't understand and determine a strategy to help themselves.

VOCABULARY

- **Is the White House a Zoo?**
  residence
  unusual
  capital

- **The Capitol Building**
  architects
  haunted
  involves

- **Arlington Heroes**
  gravesite
  recent
  tribute

Connecting Reading 5–6, SV 9781419036446

Name _____ Date _____

Monitoring Comprehension Chart

Sentence or Word I Don't Understand	What I Think It Means	How I Can Find Out	What the Sentence Means

Connecting Reading 5–6, SV 9781419036446

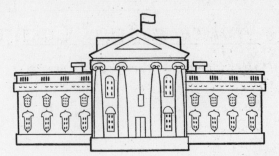

Is the White House a Zoo?

	6

Did you know that animals have lived at the White House, the **residence** of the   21

president of the United States? Some of the animals are pets that you are used to seeing.   38

However, some of them are quite **unusual**.   45

Twenty-seven presidents have had pet dogs. Ten presidents have had cats. Other   57

presidents have had ponies, hamsters, and rabbits.   64

Horses, sheep, and even elephants have walked on the White House lawn. One   77

president left flour out at night for mice that played in his bedroom!   90

Don't forget our feathered friends! Several parrots lived in the White House. So did   104

canaries, lovebirds, a goose, two bald eagles, and a turkey named Tip.   116

What were the strangest pets of all? Hippos, an alligator, and silkworms are pretty   130

strange pets! You would not expect to see those pets anywhere in our nation's **capital**!   145

 FLUENCY TIP

Be sure to phrase properly by pausing at commas.

Connecting Reading 5–6, SV 9781419036446

Name _____ Date _____

Is the White House a Zoo? Comprehension

Read each question. Darken the circle next to the correct answer.

1. What is a *residence*?

Ⓐ a place where people are buried

Ⓑ people in a neighborhood

Ⓒ the place a person lives

Ⓓ a large city

2. Which animal has NOT been a pet in the White House?

Ⓐ elephant

Ⓑ hamster

Ⓒ tiger

Ⓓ goose

3. Which animal was given flour?

Ⓐ mouse

Ⓑ dog

Ⓒ pony

Ⓓ canary

4. Why might an elephant be an unusual pet?

Ⓐ It eats hay.

Ⓑ People cannot play with it.

Ⓒ It is not an animal people in the United States keep as a pet.

Ⓓ It would crush the grass of the White House lawn.

Answer the questions using complete sentences.

5. What is the strangest pet you know? Why is it a strange pet?

_____

_____

_____

Lesson 11: It's a Capital Idea!
Connecting Reading 5–6, SV 9781419036446

Name _____   Date _____

The Capitol Building

| | 3 |

The Capitol Building is in Washington, D.C. It is the place where U.S. senators and | 18

representatives meet to make laws. It took 6 **architects** 36 years to complete the building. | 33

The Capitol is over 751 feet long. That's longer than 2 football fields. It has | 48

540 rooms, 658 windows, and 850 doorways. | 55

Some people say that the Capitol is lucky. Others think it's **haunted**! During the War | 70

of 1812, British troops set the Capitol on fire. Luckily, a sudden rainstorm put it out! In the | 88

1850s, the statue *Freedom*, which sits on top of the Capitol's dome, was being delivered on a | 105

ship. It was the only cargo to survive a storm at sea. Lucky, huh? | 119

Another legend **involves** a black cat. Believers claim that the mysterious cat shows | 132

itself right before national tragedies. | 137

The facts speak for themselves, but do you believe the stories? | 148

 FLUENCY TIP

In the sixth sentence, be sure to briefly pause after each comma.

Lesson 11: It's a Capital Idea!
Connecting Reading 5–6, SV 9781419036446

The Capitol Building Comprehension

Read each question. Darken the circle next to the correct answer.

1. What is an architect?

Ⓒ a construction worker

Ⓓ a worker in the Capitol Building

Ⓔ a person who designs buildings

Ⓕ a kind of statue

2. What is the Capitol Building used for?

Ⓒ It is where the federal laws are made.

Ⓓ People play football there.

Ⓔ Soldiers from other countries meet there.

Ⓕ Animals live there.

3. What happened to the Capitol Building in 1812?

Ⓒ A statue was delivered.

Ⓓ A ship went down.

Ⓔ The building was first designed.

Ⓕ The building was on fire.

4. Why do some people think the Capitol Building is haunted?

Ⓒ They see a mysterious black cat.

Ⓓ A British soldier walks in it.

Ⓔ A statue sits on top of the building.

Ⓕ Senators make laws there.

Answer the question using complete sentences.

5. Do you think the Capitol Building is lucky or unlucky? Explain.

_____

_____

_____

Connecting Reading 5–6, SV 9781419036446

Name _____ Date _____

Arlington Heroes

| | 2 |

There are over 260,000 people buried in Arlington National Cemetery. The cemetery is | 15

located outside of Washington, D.C. All of those buried there are soldiers. Many died while | 30

fighting for freedom. There are two former U.S. presidents buried there. They served in | 44

wars, too. | 46

Over four million people visit Arlington each year. Many look for the names of people | 61

they know. Others look for a family member who died fighting in a long-ago war. One | 78

gravesite is visited more than any other. It is the Tomb of the Unknowns. People call it | 95

"unknowns" because no one knows the names of the people buried there. Even people from | 110

recent wars are buried there. | 115

Many people also like to visit the Women in Military Service for America Memorial. It | 130

pays **tribute** to all women who have served in the U.S. military. | 142

 **FLUENCY TIP**

Remember to chunk words together into phrases that make sense together.

Name _____ Date _____

Arlington Heroes Comprehension

Read each question. Darken the circle next to the correct answer.

1. Who is buried in Arlington National Cemetery?

Ⓐ senators

Ⓑ all the presidents

Ⓒ only unknown people

Ⓓ U.S. soldiers

2. Where is Arlington National Cemetery located?

Ⓐ in Arlington, Virginia

Ⓑ outside Washington, D.C.

Ⓒ next to the White House

Ⓓ in the Women's Military Memorial

3. How did the Tomb of the Unknowns get its name?

Ⓐ No one knows in which branch of the military the people served.

Ⓑ No one knows in which war the people fought.

Ⓒ No one knows the names of the people.

Ⓓ The people buried there did not want a gravesite.

4. What does *pays tribute* mean?

Ⓐ gives money

Ⓑ gives time

Ⓒ shows honor

Ⓓ asks for help

Answer the question using complete sentences.

5. Why do you think so many people visit Arlington National Cemetery?

_____

_____

_____

Lesson 11: It's a Capital Idea!
Connecting Reading 5–6, SV 9781419036446

Lesson 12: Getting from Here to There

Connecting Background

LEVELED TITLES

- *The Erie Canal — 5.0*
- *The Mississippi Steamboats — 6.3*
- *The Cumberland Road — 7.1*

Theme Notes

Transportation has always been an important part of America's growth and development. Early settlers walked, paddled canoes, or rode horses when they traveled. To move west, they rode in wagons on roads they cleared through the forests and across mountains. Eventually, steamboats and trains were the easiest methods to travel from place to place. This lesson looks at some of the paths on which people in the United States traveled—the Erie Canal, the Cumberland Road, and the Mississippi River.

Fluency Focus: Word Accuracy

To read fluently and smoothly, readers need to say words accurately. Fluent readers learn all the words in a selection. They learn how to pronounce them and what the words mean. They look in advance for difficult words, especially names of people and place names.

Fluency Practice

Write this sentence on the board: *The transcontinental railroad started in Omaha, Nebraska.*

Invite a volunteer to underline the difficult words. Say each underlined word and tell its meaning. Then have partners take turns reading the sentence fluently.

VOCABULARY

- **The Erie Canal**
  doubtful
  tough
  congratulations

- **The Mississippi Steamboats**
  approached
  ledge
  entertainers

- **The Cumberland Road**
  options
  preferred
  spectacular

Comprehension Focus: Problem and Solution

A problem is something that causes trouble. People have to find a way to fix, or solve, the problem. They work to find solutions to the problem. Sometimes there are several problems that need to be solved. One solution may work for all the problems, or several solutions may fix the same problem. As students read the selections, have them complete the Problem and Solution Chart on page 97 to show the solutions to the problems.

Name _____ Date _____

Problem and Solution Chart

Title _____

Problem 1	Solution

Problem 2	Solution

Problem 3	Solution

Problem 4	Solution

Problem 5	Solution

Lesson 12: Getting from Here to There
Connecting Reading 5–6, SV 9781419036446

The Erie Canal

3

In 1817, it was faster and cheaper to travel by water than by road. Therefore, — 18

New Yorkers decided to connect Lake Erie and the Hudson River with a canal. The — 33

Erie Canal would be 363 miles long. It would need 83 locks. A lock is used to raise — 51

or lower the water level. — 56

Some people were **doubtful** that the canal could be built. It certainly was a challenge. — 71

The **tough** work was done with horses, mules, and wagons. Thousands of workers used only — 86

hand tools to clear the way and dig the canal. — 96

The Erie Canal was finished in 1825. Cannons had been placed every ten miles. At the — 112

opening they were fired one after another. It was as if they were saying, "**Congratulations**, — 127

workers! You can be proud of the canal!" — 135

⚙ FLUENCY TIP

Remember not to skip words. Practice difficult words until you can read smoothly.

Connecting Reading 5–6, SV 9781419036446

The Erie Canal Comprehension

Read each question. Darken the circle next to the correct answer.

1. What was the fastest way to travel in 1817?

Ⓐ boat

Ⓑ horse

Ⓒ car

Ⓓ train

2. What is a canal?

Ⓐ a road between two rivers

Ⓑ a track for a train

Ⓒ a bridge over a river

Ⓓ a waterway made by people

3. What can you conclude about making the canal?

Ⓐ It was completed in a short time.

Ⓑ Clearing the land was easy.

Ⓒ It was hard work.

Ⓓ There was lots of fighting.

4. Why did the people use cannons?

Ⓐ to celebrate the canal being completed

Ⓑ to scare away robbers

Ⓒ to help the workers dig faster

Ⓓ to clear the trees

Answer the question using complete sentences.

5. Why did people build the Erie Canal?

_____

_____

_____

Connecting Reading 5–6, SV 9781419036446

Name _____   Date _____

The Mississippi Steamboats

	3

Each steamboat that traveled the Mississippi River had its own special whistle. The   16
steamboat would blow its whistle as it **approached** a town. Some children knew each boat   31
by its whistle. Often, they would play on a **ledge** over the river and hear the boat coming.   49

The arrival of a steamboat was an important event. It brought the mail, clothing, food,   64
furniture, and books. Sometimes **entertainers** were on the boat, and they would stop and   78
do a show. As the children shouted and raced for the landing, the whole town would follow.   95

A steamboat could easily travel along a river. A trip that would have taken six months   111
in a boat without an engine took only six days in a steamboat.   124

Steamboats on the Mississippi River were stopped during the Civil War in the 1860s.   138
Although travel by steamboat recovered somewhat after the war, the railroads soon took   151
away much of the steamboats' business.   157

 FLUENCY TIP

Read this like you are an expert on the topic.

The Mississippi Steamboats Comprehension

Read each question. Darken the circle next to the correct answer.

1. How did people know which steamboat was docking?

Ⓐ They read the names on the steamboats.

Ⓑ The steamboat captain yelled out the name.

Ⓒ Each steamboat had its own whistle.

Ⓓ People knew when the steamboat would arrive.

2. Why were steamboats important to people?

Ⓐ They brought mail.

Ⓑ They sold food.

Ⓒ People could play on them.

Ⓓ People could race with them.

3. Which is an entertainer?

Ⓐ a firefighter

Ⓑ a soldier

Ⓒ a clown

Ⓓ an astronaut

4. Why did the steamboats stop during the Civil War?

Ⓐ The river dried up.

Ⓑ Armies fought on the river.

Ⓒ The steamboats were too old.

Ⓓ The captains became soldiers.

Answer the question using complete sentences.

5. Why did the whole town come to see the steamboat when it docked?

_____

_____

_____

www.harcourtschoolsupply.com
101
Lesson 12: Getting from Here to There
Connecting Reading 5–6, SV 9781419036446

The Cumberland Road

People in the early 1800s had a variety of **options** for their mode of transportation.   3 / 18

They could travel by boat, horse, or horse and wagon. Most people **preferred** to travel by   34

boat because that was the quickest and smoothest way.   43

The Cumberland Road was built to connect two busy waterways. The road started   56

in Cumberland, Maryland, at the Potomac River and followed an American Indian trail   69

westward. It ended in Wheeling, West Virginia, on the Ohio River. Travelers could then sail   84

down the Ohio River to lands in the Midwest.   93

The Cumberland Road was the first highway between states. The road was about 130   107

miles long and built of crushed stone. The road began to fall apart fairly quickly. However,   123

the bridges that were part of the road were **spectacular**!   133

⚙ FLUENCY TIP

Practice pronouncing the place names and vocabulary words before you read
this aloud.

Connecting Reading 5–6, SV 9781419036446

The Cumberland Road Comprehension

Read each question. Darken the circle next to the correct answer.

1. What was the preferred way to travel in the 1800s?

Ⓐ boat

Ⓑ horse

Ⓒ horse and wagon

Ⓓ on foot

2. What did the Cumberland Road connect?

Ⓐ two towns

Ⓑ two waterways

Ⓒ two houses

Ⓓ two colonies

3. Why was the road important?

Ⓐ It was really long.

Ⓑ It followed a river.

Ⓒ It was made of crushed stone.

Ⓓ It was the first highway between states.

4. If a bridge is *spectacular*, what is it like?

Ⓐ poorly built

Ⓑ beautiful to look at

Ⓒ really tall

Ⓓ made of stone

Answer the question using complete sentences.

5. Why do you think the road may have started to fall apart soon after it was built?

_____

_____

_____

Lesson 13: Dig It!
Connecting Background

Theme Notes

An archaeologist is a person who studies the lives and customs of ancient humans. A paleontologist studies ancient animals. These scientists carefully dig in the ground to uncover bones or other clues that tell more about the time period. This lesson focuses on three important sites—the ruins of Pompeii, a dinosaur discovery, and prehistoric artifacts in the country of Laos.

Fluency Focus: Punctuation

Fluent readers pay attention to punctuation to help them understand and remember what they read. They pause at commas, raise their voice for question marks, and show excitement at exclamation points. If a word is italicized, boldfaced, or in all uppercase letters, they say it with emphasis.

Fluency Practice

Write these words on the board: *Look at what I've found I was digging here and I found a piece of a bone it looks like a T. rex bone*

Have students write the words, adding punctuation correctly. Then have them practice reading the sentences fluently.

Comprehension Focus: Drawing Conclusions

A conclusion is a judgment that makes sense. To draw a conclusion that is reasonable, readers must look at the details in the text. Then they have to think about what they already know. By putting all the information together, readers can understand ideas that are not directly stated. Students will be able to draw conclusions using the Drawing Conclusions Chart on page 105.

VOCABULARY

- *Pompeii*
  attracted
  extravagant
  artifacts

- *Jane*
  paleontologists
  astounding
  serrated

- *The Plain of Jars*
  prehistoric
  archaeologist
  artifacts

Name _____ Date _____

Drawing Conclusions Chart

Conclusion	Details from the Article

Connecting Reading 5–6, SV 9781419036446

Pompeii

| | 1 |

Summer in Pompeii* was lovely. Its sandy beaches **attracted** many visitors. Rich | 13

Romans built **extravagant** homes there. That all ended on August 24, A.D. 79. | 26

A volcano erupted and destroyed Pompeii that day. When it blew, gas and steam shot | 41

into the air, and three-inch stones flew into the sky. Ash fell on the town for two days. | 59

Some people were lucky and escaped on the first day. Those who stayed in the city | 75

died. When the volcano calmed and the debris in the air settled, Pompeii lay under twenty | 91

feet of stones and ash. The city was never rebuilt. | 101

Later, in 1748, the king of Naples had workers begin digging in Pompeii. It was a huge | 118

job to uncover the ruins. Over the years, workers have found homes, shops, schools, theaters, | 133

and other **artifacts**. The work still continues to this day. These objects have taught us about | 149

the people of Pompeii and how they lived. | 157

* (pom PAY)

⚙ FLUENCY TIP

Watch for commas in the last paragraph. Make sure to pause at each comma.

Name _____ Date _____

Pompeii Comprehension

Read each question. Darken the circle next to the correct answer.

1. What happened to destroy Pompeii?

    Ⓐ A tsunami hit.

    Ⓑ A volcano erupted.

    Ⓒ An earthquake struck.

    Ⓓ No one knows.

2. Why did the Romans probably choose not to rebuild the city?

    Ⓐ The city was covered with ash and debris.

    Ⓑ People were happy where they were.

    Ⓒ They forgot about it.

    Ⓓ There was no way to get there.

3. What did scientists find in Pompeii?

    Ⓐ swimming pools

    Ⓑ theaters

    Ⓒ restaurants

    Ⓓ offices

4. What can you conclude about the city of Pompeii?

    Ⓐ It was easy to uncover.

    Ⓑ It had lots of plants.

    Ⓒ It was poor.

    Ⓓ It was big.

Answer the question using complete sentences.

5. Describe what the city looked like after the disaster.

_____

_____

_____

Lesson 13: Dig It!

Connecting Reading 5–6, SV 9781419036446

Jane

	1

In 2001, a group of **paleontologists** traveled to Montana to look for dinosaur bones. **15**
They were from a very small museum in Rockford, Illinois. On their final day, they made **31**
an **astounding** discovery. A toe and a leg bone were sticking out of a dry creek bank. The **49**
scientists carefully dug up the bones and took them back to their museum. The team knew **65**
the bones were from a dinosaur, but they didn't know which kind. They spent the next **81**
months obtaining permits to continue the dig. **88**

The following summer, the team returned to the site and made two more important **102**
discoveries. They found a lower jawbone and **serrated** teeth. These bones could only **115**
belong to one of two types of dinosaurs. After paleontologists spent more than 10,000 hours **130**
digging, the quest was over. They had found the most complete, best-preserved, young **143**
Tyrannosaurus rex ever discovered. The team named her "Jane." **152**

 **FLUENCY TIP**

Read the next-to-last sentence fluently by pausing at the commas.

Jane Comprehension

Read each question. Darken the circle next to the correct answer.

1. What is Jane?

Ⓐ a dinosaur

Ⓑ a museum

Ⓒ a paleontologist

Ⓓ a book

2. Where was Jane found?

Ⓐ Illinois

Ⓑ Montana

Ⓒ South Dakota

Ⓓ Wyoming

3. What helped identify Jane?

Ⓐ a leg bone

Ⓑ serrated teeth

Ⓒ a permit

Ⓓ a map

4. What happened after the scientists found the first bones?

Ⓐ They got permits.

Ⓑ They gave up.

Ⓒ They left them there.

Ⓓ They went to a new site.

Answer the question using complete sentences.

5. Why is this discovery so important to a museum and to the scientific world?

_____

_____

_____

The Plain of Jars

| | 4 |

Laos is a small country that lies next to Vietnam. During the Vietnam War, Laos was | 20

bombed more times than anywhere else, even though it never participated in the war. Thirty | 35

years later, hundreds of unexploded bombs can still be found in the country's high plains. | 50

But so can something else—giant **prehistoric** jars made of sandstone. | 61

In the mid-1930s, an **archaeologist** from France first studied the "Plain of Jars." So far, | 76

over 60 of these areas have been discovered, some with over 200 jars. Other **artifacts** were | 92

found at the dig sites as well. From their studies, archaeologists believe that the jars were used | 109

for burials between 1,500 and 2,000 years ago. However, no one knows who made the jars | 125

or how they got there. | 130

Some of the jars stand upright, while some have fallen on their sides. The tallest are | 146

almost ten feet high and weigh several tons. Surprisingly, while the jars can be found in | 162

some of the most highly bombed areas of Laos, many of them are completely intact! | 177

⚙️ FLUENCY TIP

A long dash is a punctuation mark that signals you to pause briefly.

The Plain of Jars Comprehension

Read each question. Darken the circle next to the correct answer.

1. Why did Laos most likely get bombed?

Ⓐ Laos was fighting Vietnam.

Ⓑ The pilots missed their targets.

Ⓒ People in the country were fighting each other.

Ⓓ It was a way to keep people from coming to Laos.

2. Why do scientists call the area they found the "Plain of Jars"?

Ⓐ The jars are not decorated.

Ⓑ The ground often shakes.

Ⓒ Fields are filled with jars.

Ⓓ The jars are in plain view.

3. What do scientists think the jars were used for?

Ⓐ holding bombs

Ⓑ food storage

Ⓒ building houses

Ⓓ burying people

4. What surprised the scientists?

Ⓐ They don't know who made the jars.

Ⓑ Many jars did not get hurt during the bombing.

Ⓒ The jars are in Laos.

Ⓓ The jars were so old.

Answer the question using complete sentences.

5. How do you think the jars remained intact after all the bombing?

_____

_____

_____

Lesson 14: Exciting Energy
Connecting Background

LEVELED TITLES

- *Wind Powers a School* — 5.4
- *Using the Sun's Heat* — 6.4
- *Lowell National Historical Park* — 7.4

Theme Notes

Everything has some kind of energy. Energy is never lost or made, but it can change. Here on Earth, everyone uses, sees, or feels energy every day. This lesson focuses on three kinds of energy—wind power, solar energy, and water power.

Fluency Focus: Phrasing

Fluent readers pay attention to the phrases, or word groups, in each sentence so that they read faster and more smoothly. A phrase is a group of words that act together to make a whole thought. Chunking, or reading forward through several words at a time, can help students read more fluently.

Fluency Practice

Write this sentence on the board: *Rio will carefully research different kinds of energy, including solar, wind, and water, for his project.*

Ask students to write the sentence and use slashes to show the phrasing. Then have them read the words in each word group without pausing.

Comprehension Focus: Steps in a Process

A process is a way to do something. Steps explain the order in which the process happens. Words like *first*, *next*, *last*, and *finally* clarify the order of the steps. The Step Chart on page 113 can help students understand the order of steps in the processes presented in the articles.

VOCABULARY

- *Wind Powers a School*
  generate
  turbine
  generator

- *Using the Sun's Heat*
  antifreeze
  exchanger
  absorb

- *Lowell National Historical Park*
  purchasing
  turbine
  mechanical
    engineering

Name _____ Date _____

Step Chart

Process_____

Step 1

Step 2

Step 3

Step 4

Step 5

Step 6

Lesson 14: Exciting Energy
Connecting Reading 5–6, SV 9781419036446

Wind Powers a School

	4

Lee is proud of his school in Spirit Lake, Iowa. He likes to explain something special | 20 |
to visitors. It is the first U.S. school to use wind to **generate** electricity. | 34 |

A giant wind **turbine** was built to power the elementary school. It makes enough | 48 |
electricity for everything in the building. | 54 |

Now a second, larger turbine is nearby. It makes electricity for all the other school | 69 |
buildings and the football-field lights. | 74 |

The turbine blades are high up, where winds are stronger. When the wind turns the | 89 |
blades, the blades cause other parts in the turbine to spin. These parts make the **generator** | 105 |
run. The generator makes electricity. A brake stops the blades in bad storms. | 118 |

⚙️ **FLUENCY TIP**

You say the words of a phrase together when you talk. Do that as you read each phrase, too.

114

Wind Powers a School Comprehension

Read each question. Darken the circle next to the correct answer.

1. Why is Lee's school special?

 Ⓐ Students teach math.

 Ⓑ Wind powers the school.

 Ⓒ Students build turbines.

 Ⓓ Students play football.

2. What does the first turbine do?

 Ⓐ It makes electricity for the school building.

 Ⓑ It makes electricity for the football field.

 Ⓒ It turns the blades on another turbine.

 Ⓓ It stops the turbine from turning.

3. Why are the turbine blades high in the air?

 Ⓐ The blades need to be above the school.

 Ⓑ The generator is there.

 Ⓒ They are too big to put on the ground.

 Ⓓ They need to be where the wind is strongest.

4. What happens just before the generator runs?

 Ⓐ The brakes stop the blades.

 Ⓑ Parts inside the turbine spin.

 Ⓒ The blades spin.

 Ⓓ The wind blows.

Answer the questions using complete sentences.

5. Do you think more schools should use wind energy? Why or why not?

_____

_____

_____

Lesson 14: Exciting Energy
Connecting Reading 5–6, SV 9781419036446

Using the Sun's Heat

4

Grandpa and Adela have everything they need to assemble a solar water heater. They   18
know that conservation of natural resources is very important. So using the sun's energy   32
will help their family and Earth.   38

In the basement, Grandpa and Adela first install a water tank that has pipes filled with   54
antifreeze, a fluid that won't freeze in winter. A heat **exchanger** machine is inside, too.   69

Next, Adela holds the ladder as Grandpa fastens two solar panels on the roof. The   84
panels face south to catch as much sunlight as possible. The panels are black to best **absorb**   101
the sun's heat energy. Small pipes inside the panels are filled with antifreeze.   114

Grandpa connects pipes from the panels to a pump and then to the water tank. The   130
sun-heated fluid heats the water. The fluid is then pumped back up into the solar panels for   147
reheating. Energy keeps moving!   151

⚙ FLUENCY TIP

Try to read smoothly, moving through each phrase without stopping long.

Name _____ Date _____

Using the Sun's Heat Comprehension

Read each question. Darken the circle next to the correct answer.

1. Why is Grandpa putting in a solar heater?

    Ⓐ to help conserve energy

    Ⓑ to make electricity

    Ⓒ to get water in the house

    Ⓓ to heat the house

2. Which is NOT needed for a solar water heater?

    Ⓐ antifreeze

    Ⓑ panels

    Ⓒ water tank

    Ⓓ gas pump

3. Why does Grandpa put panels on the south side of the house?

    Ⓐ He doesn't want the water in the pipes to freeze.

    Ⓑ They will collect more heat there.

    Ⓒ He can reach that part of the roof more easily.

    Ⓓ The pipes are there already.

4. Why do some pipes need antifreeze?

    Ⓐ It is needed to help heat the water.

    Ⓑ It keeps the water heated all the time.

    Ⓒ If the water freezes in the pipes, they might break.

    Ⓓ The hot water cannot go back into the panels.

Answer the questions using complete sentences.

5. Could all homes have a solar water heater? Why or why not?

_____

_____

_____

Lesson 14: Exciting Energy

Connecting Reading 5–6, SV 9781419036446

Name _____ Date _____

Lowell National Historical Park

| | 4 |

Jeff's family will visit an important park in Lowell, Massachusetts, next week. They | 17
will see where water power helped to change U.S. manufacturing in the 1800s. | 30

Jeff surfed the Web to research the history of Lowell. He discovered that the young | 45
United States wanted to manufacture products instead of **purchasing** them from Britain. | 57
People processing cloth by hand could not supply the rising demand. | 68

A power loom was a new invention that could weave cloth much more quickly. Francis | 83
Cabot Lowell constructed many power loom machines. He then built ten buildings, called | 96
mills, to house them. Lowell had miles of canals dug to bring water to the mills. The force | 114
of the running water would turn wheels, causing a **turbine** to spin. That energy powered | 129
hundreds of these loom machines. | 134

Although Jeff isn't very interested in the historical part of the trip, he certainly wants | 149
to view the turbines and looms. Jeff likes anything related to **mechanical engineering**. | 162

⚙️ **FLUENCY TIP**

Remember to keep reading forward phrase by phrase. If a sentence doesn't make sense, reread the phrases carefully.

Lowell National Historical Park Comprehension

Read each question. Darken the circle next to the correct answer.

1. What is Lowell National Historical Park?

Ⓐ a park to camp in

Ⓑ an old factory

Ⓒ a place to go fishing

Ⓓ a factory that makes clothing

2. Why is the park important?

Ⓐ It used water power.

Ⓑ It was the first factory to make clothing.

Ⓒ It was an engineering school.

Ⓓ It had ten buildings.

3. Why did Lowell build power looms?

Ⓐ He wanted to create a park.

Ⓑ He needed to put them into buildings.

Ⓒ He needed canals for water.

Ⓓ He wanted to make cloth faster.

4. Why did Jeff read about Lowell on the Web?

Ⓐ He is researching a school project.

Ⓑ He likes to learn how mechanical things work.

Ⓒ His family is going there.

Ⓓ His family owns the factory.

Answer the question using complete sentences.

5. What would you like to learn during a visit to Lowell?

_____

_____

_____

Connecting Reading 5–6, SV 9781419036446

Lesson 15: Secrets in Stone
Connecting Background

Theme Notes

People throughout history have used the materials around them to make monuments. Stone has long been the choice of these builders. Not only is it easily available, it lasts for centuries. This lesson highlights famous stones, including the Rosetta Stone, the stone rings of Stonehenge, and the stone statues on Easter Island.

Fluency Focus: Expression

Fluent readers read with expression. This is important because it makes reading more interesting and can help improve understanding. The reader can stress certain words in order to read with more expression. Often punctuation can help. However, sometimes the reader will have to decide how to read with expression based on the purpose of the sentence.

Fluency Practice

Write these sentences on the board: *Look at the beautiful writing on that stone! What tools did they use to make the letters and shapes?*

Encourage students to read the sentences with the proper expression.

Comprehension Focus: Main Idea and Supporting Details

The main idea is the most important idea in a selection. It tells what the selection is mainly about. A selection can have one main idea. Paragraphs and different parts of the selection can have main ideas, too. Reading titles can help a reader determine the main idea. The graphic organizer on page 121 can help students identify the main idea and supporting details of their selections.

VOCABULARY

- *Easter Island*
  archaeologists
  platforms
  diligently

- *Rosetta Stone*
  decipher
  hieroglyphic
  compiled

- *Stonehenge*
  archaeologists
  erected
  unexplainable

Name _____ Date _____

Main Idea and Supporting Details
Graphic Organizer

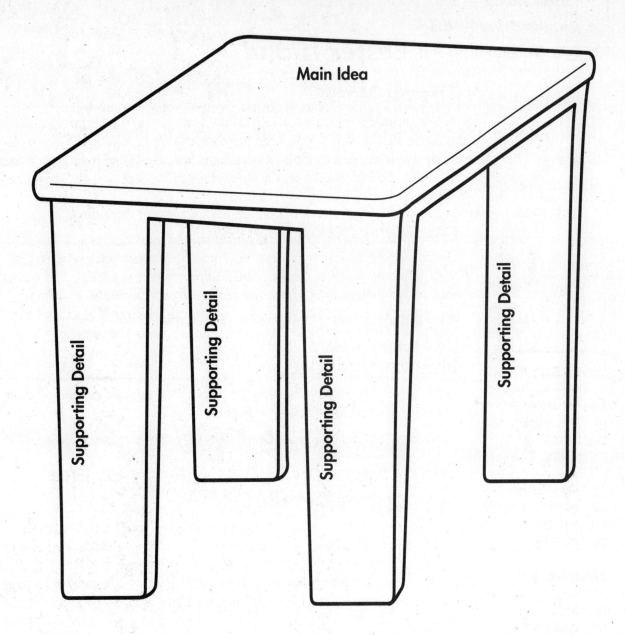

Lesson 15: Secrets in Stone
Connecting Reading 5–6, SV 9781419036446

Name _____   Date _____

Easter Island

2
18
33
49
54
67
87
93
108
121
129

Easter Island is in the South Pacific Ocean. It covers about 64 square miles. It is far away from places where other people live. Europeans first found the island on Easter Sunday in 1722. That is how the island got its name. However, other people had lived there for over 1,000 years.

Archaeologists have found almost 900 statues on the island. Most of them range from 11 to 20 feet tall. A few are taller than 30 feet. Imagine how big they look to a man who is 6 feet tall!

The artists used stone picks to carve the statues from volcanic rock. Then the islanders moved some statues onto raised **platforms**. The statues were important to the people, so they must have worked **diligently** on them.

⚙️ **FLUENCY TIP**

To practice reading with expression, reread the second paragraph to a partner. Remember to look at the punctuation and purpose of each sentence. Find words to stress.

Easter Island Comprehension

Read each question. Darken the circle next to the correct answer.

1. How did the island get its name?

Ⓐ People living there had a huge feast on Easter Sunday.

Ⓑ The people living there were the Eastern Tribe.

Ⓒ The statues were found on Easter Sunday.

Ⓓ The island was discovered on Easter Sunday.

2. How many statues are on the island?

Ⓐ 1,000

Ⓑ 900

Ⓒ 1,722

Ⓓ 64

3. How do diligent people work?

Ⓐ lazily

Ⓑ poorly

Ⓒ steadily

Ⓓ sloppily

4. What is the main idea of the article?

Ⓐ how the island got its name

Ⓑ amazing old statues

Ⓒ an archaeologist's job

Ⓓ how to make stone statues

Answer the question using complete sentences.

5. Imagine the island is changing its name. What should its new name be? Explain your choice.

_____

_____

_____

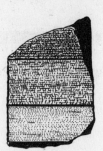

Rosetta Stone

	2
The Rosetta Stone was discovered in 1799 in Egypt. Carved in 196 B.C., the stone	17
contains the same text in three writing systems and in two languages, Egyptian and Greek.	32
An Englishman and a Frenchman worked to **decipher** the writing on the Rosetta Stone. The	47
Englishman looked at the direction the **hieroglyphic** birds and animals faced. This told him	61
which way to read the writing.	67

The Rosetta Stone was discovered in 1799 in Egypt. Carved in 196 B.C., the stone contains the same text in three writing systems and in two languages, Egyptian and Greek. An Englishman and a Frenchman worked to **decipher** the writing on the Rosetta Stone. The Englishman looked at the direction the **hieroglyphic** birds and animals faced. This told him which way to read the writing.

They also used the Greek writing as a guide to understand the hieroglyphics. Egyptian hieroglyphics had been a mystery for many years. The Frenchman showed that the hieroglyphics represented sounds. He **compiled** a list of hieroglyphic signs that equaled Greek letters.

The Rosetta Stone has an interesting shape. It is made of dark gray rock called granite. It is about 3 feet 9 inches long, 2 feet 4 inches wide, and 11 inches thick. Part of the top and right side are missing. The stone is now located in a museum in England.

Line counts:
81, 94, 106, 108, 124, 146, 160

⚙ FLUENCY TIP

You can read nonfiction with expression. First, read the first sentence in the second paragraph without expression. Then, read it again stressing the words *Greek* and *understand*.

Rosetta Stone Comprehension

Read each question. Darken the circle next to the correct answer.

1. How many languages are on the Rosetta Stone?

Ⓐ two

Ⓑ nine

Ⓒ three

Ⓓ six

2. How did the scientists know how to read the writing?

Ⓐ The words were Greek, so it was read like Greek.

Ⓑ The animals faced in one direction, so they read it in that direction.

Ⓒ The shape told how to read it.

Ⓓ It was in French, so the French scientist could read it.

3. What is *hieroglyphics*?

Ⓐ ancient picture writing

Ⓑ ancient Greek words

Ⓒ interesting words

Ⓓ letters written backward

4. What is the main idea of this article?

Ⓐ ancient stones and how they were made

Ⓑ how the Rosetta Stone was made

Ⓒ the Rosetta Stone and the discovery of what the writing means

Ⓓ who discovered the Rosetta Stone

Answer the question using complete sentences.

5. What impact did deciphering the Rosetta Stone have on our knowledge of ancient Egypt?

_____

_____

_____

Stonehenge

	1

Stonehenge, a mysterious monument in England, consists of large stones set in circles.   14
Archaeologists believe that ancient people built Stonehenge and used it as a gathering place.   28
First built around 3100 B.C., the site today lies in ruins. Many of the stones have fallen or   46
have been destroyed by early modern builders or weather.   55

Stonehenge was built in three stages. In Stonehenge I, people used deer antlers as picks   70
and ox shoulder blades as shovels to carve a circular ditch about 320 feet in diameter. They   87
erected wooden posts in a circle.   93

Then, about 500 to 600 years later, people began to rebuild in stone. They set some   109
stones in a circle, but for some **unexplainable** reason, never finished the task.   122

Another 200 years passed before they began working again. They brought giant   134
sandstone rocks 20 miles. They stood stones up and laid stones across the tops. They created   150
a circle and a horseshoe. The remains of these can still be seen today.   164

In 1922, the British government started to restore Stonehenge. It is one of the United   179
Kingdom's most popular tourist attractions. Over one million people visit the site each year.   193

⚙️ FLUENCY TIP

When reading with expression, remember to pause when needed. Read the second
paragraph to a partner with and without pausing. Listen to the difference.

Lesson 15: Secrets in Stone
Connecting Reading 5–6, SV 9781419036446

Name _____ Date _____

Stonehenge Comprehension

Read each question. Darken the circle next to the correct answer.

1. What is one reason that Stonehenge is in ruins?

Ⓐ Weather knocked over the stones.

Ⓑ An earthquake knocked over the stones.

Ⓒ The sun cracked the stones in two.

Ⓓ People carried the stones away.

2. What was Stonehenge like at first?

Ⓐ It was made of stone.

Ⓑ It was made of bone.

Ⓒ It was made of wood.

Ⓓ It was shaped like a horseshoe.

3. What can visitors see today?

Ⓐ only a ditch

Ⓑ a circle with large stones

Ⓒ wooden posts

Ⓓ an unfinished circle of stones

4. Which sentence from the article tells the main idea?

Ⓐ *Stonehenge, a mysterious monument in England, consists of large stones set in circles.*

Ⓑ *Archaeologists believe that ancient people built Stonehenge and used it as a gathering place.*

Ⓒ *Stonehenge was built in three stages.*

Ⓓ *It is one of the United Kingdom's most popular tourist attractions.*

Answer the question using complete sentences.

5. Why do you think so many people visit Stonehenge?

_____

_____

_____

Connecting Reading 5–6, SV 9781419036446

Answer Key

Page 11
1. D 2. A 3. B 4. C
5. Answers will vary.

Page 13
1. B 2. D 3. B 4. A
5. The crow was sure that his destiny was to be great and powerful.

Page 15
1. C 2. A 3. A 4. B
5. Answers will vary.

Page 19
1. C 2. A 3. B 4. A
5. I can wash my hands frequently to help keep from getting a cold. Germs are on everything I touch, so if I wash, the germs will go away.

Page 21
1. C 2. B 3. D 4. B
5. Cooking food kills germs.

Page 23
1. B 2. C 3. B 4. D
5. Superheroes are people who do good things to help people. Bacteria do good things for people, so the author is comparing bacteria to superheroes.

Page 27
1. B 2. C 3. C 4. D
5. Answers will vary.

Page 29
1. D 2. D 3. C 4. A
5. There is more support in the center of the house, so it is less likely for the house to fall down or the roof to blow away. Also, there probably are no windows in the center of the house.

Page 31
1. C 2. B 3. C 4. A
5. Answers will vary.

Page 35
1. C 2. B 3. D 4. B
5. Answers will vary.

Page 37
1. C 2. A 3. D 4. A
5. Possible answer: The nervous system controls sight, so if the eyes did not work, then you could not see.

Page 39
1. B 2. C 3. B 4. A
5. Most likely answer: Food should be chosen for its nutritional value because the body will stay healthy and work better if it gets the nutrients it needs.

Page 43
1. B 2. A 3. C 4. A
5. Qiviut keeps them warm in the winter, and big hooves break ice and dig in snow to find water and food.

Page 45
1. B 2. B 3. D 4. B
5. The glacier got rid of all the plant life. As it melted, the plant life started to grow again.

Page 47
1. C 2. B 3. D 4. C
5. Most likely answer: Different temperatures and weather conditions might affect what the lights look like.

Page 51
1. C 2. B 3. A 4. C
5. Most likely answer: The land around the Arctic Circle must be brown and gray because the fur of arctic foxes is brown or gray in the summer.

Page 53
1. B 2. A 3. A 4. C
5. The claws are long and sharp because anteaters keep them protected when they walk, and they use them to fight other animals.

Page 55
1. C 2. A 3. A 4. A
5. Possible answers: They are camouflaged from their prey. They are good swimmers and climbers. They can run up to 35 miles per hour.

Page 59
1. A 2. B 3. C 4. D
5. The supplies needed were a knife, jars, salt, linen, charms, jewels, a sheet, the Book of the Dead, wax, and perfume.

Page 61
1. C 2. A 3. B 4. A
5. Answers will vary.

Page 63
1. C 2. B 3. C 4. C
5. Possible answer: They can look at the clothes to see what people wore, and they can look at the furniture, weapons, and chariot to see how they lived.

Page 67
1. D 2. B 3. A 4. C
5. Answers will vary.

Page 69
1. B 2. B 3. D 4. A
5. Answers will vary.

Page 71
1. D 2. C 3. D 4. C
5. Most likely answer: The river was red from the rocks and sand it carried.

Page 75
1. A 2. B 3. A 4. D
5. President Roosevelt was kind and liked nature, because he let a bear cub free so it would not be killed.

Page 77
1. D 2. A 3. B 4. B
5. Reading aloud allows you to practice fluent reading, so you can develop expression, word accuracy, and phrasing.

Page 79
1. A 2. A 3. C 4. C
5. Answers will vary.

Page 83
1. B 2. C 3. A 4. D
5. Possible answer: People are more likely to talk to others who are like them. People who were poor would talk to Eva because they thought she was poor.

Page 85
1. B 2. A 3. C 4. A
5. Answers will vary.

Page 87
1. B 2. A 3. D 4. A
5. Answers will vary.

Page 91
1. C 2. C 3. A 4. C
5. Answers will vary.

Page 93
1. C 2. A 3. D 4. A
5. Answers will vary.

Page 95
1. D 2. B 3. C 4. C
5. Answers will vary.

Page 99
1. A 2. D 3. C 4. A
5. It would be cheaper and faster to transport goods and people by boat.

Page 101
1. C 2. A 3. C 4. B
5. Possible answer: Small towns did not have much contact with the outside world, so people were interested to hear the news, get the mail, and see if an entertainer was on board.

Page 103
1. A 2. B 3. D 4. B
5. Answers will vary.

Page 107
1. B 2. A 3. B 4. D
5. Answers will vary.

Page 109
1. A 2. B 3. B 4. A
5. Possible answer: The scientists would be able to learn more about the *Tyrannosaurus rex* by looking at the bones.

Page 111
1. B 2. C 3. D 4. B
5. Answers will vary.

Page 115
1. B 2. A 3. D 4. B
5. Answers will vary.

Page 117
1. A 2. D 3. B 4. C
5. Most likely answer: All homes could not have a solar water heater because they may not be in an area that gets lots of sun.

Page 119
1. B 2. A 3. D 4. C
5. Answers will vary.

Page 123
1. D 2. B 3. C 4. B
5. Answers will vary.

Page 125
1. A 2. B 3. A 4. C
5. The scientists used the writing on the stone to unlock the meaning of all Egyptian hieroglyphics.

Page 127
1. A 2. C 3. B 4. A
5. Answers will vary.

Answer Key
Connecting Reading 5–6, SV 9781419036446